Milligan, dr[...] road in Italy, spotted Seco[...] y did a sharp left-hander i[...] o the Bridge'. Spike, anxi[...] n hot pursuit. Unknown to [...] only one half of the bridge and had laid a smoke [...] disguise the fact from the enemy. Secombe went through the smoke in top gear. Milligan, hearing the splash, stopped inches from the edge, just in time to see Harry's dripping head pop up. 'He was livid,' recalls Milligan, 'and asked a very rude question about the rest of the bridge ...'

Top BBC producer Roy Speer got a phone call. A rich, plummy voice familiar to millions of radio listeners said: 'This is Kenneth Horne. I've got Dickie Murdoch with me. We saw a fellow the other night who might be good for your show. A most amusing impersonator – didn't you agree, Dickie?'

Another familiar voice, apparently on the extension phone, concurred: 'Oh, absolutely. First rate.'

'What's his name?' asked Speer.

'Peter Sellers.'

Speer wrote the name down.

Then a third voice said: 'Actually, I'm Peter Sellers ...'

Secombe's shaving act died the death in Bolton, and Harry caught the next train. He sent Bentine a telegram: AUDIENCE WITH ME ALL THE WAY STOP MANAGED TO SHAKE THEM OFF AT THE STATION ...

The Story of the Goons is as hilarious and zany as The Goon Show itself!

ALFRED DRAPER is the author of a number of fiction and non-fiction books. His *Swansong for a Rare Bird* was runner-up in the Macmillan/Panther crime novel competition. *The Death Penalty* which lifted the lid off soccer violence was a bestseller here and abroad. *Smoke Without Fire* recounted the historical fight of Lieut.-Commander Swabe to clear his name of an indecency charge.

The Prince of Wales spotlighted the scandals surrounding the heir to the throne and the pleasure-bent Marlborough House Set during Victoria's reign.

Draper is a former journalist with the *Daily Express*. During his many years with the newspaper he specialized in crime reporting and covered a number of now-famous trials. As a foreign correspondent he travelled to numerous parts of the world covering wars and major disasters. Married with two children, he lives in Herts.

He was ably assisted during the research of this book by authors John Austin and Harry Edgington.

The Story of The Goons

ALFRED DRAPER

with

JOHN AUSTIN

and

HARRY EDGINGTON

EVEREST BOOKS LIMITED
4 Valentine Place, London, SE1

Published in Great Britain by Everest Books Ltd, 1976

A paperback original

ISBN 0905018 257

Copyright © Austin – Draper – Edgington 1976

Printed in Great Britain by
Richard Clay (The Chaucer Press), Ltd.,
Bungay, Suffolk

CONTENTS

ACKNOWLEDGEMENTS

Anyone writing about The Goons finds himself in the unusual but enviable position of having a surfeit of readily-available material. The relieved researcher doesn't have to burrow into dusty archives for slender clues or leads, for thousands upon thousands of words have been written about Spike, Harry and Peter, and the wonderful gallery of characters they created. Furthermore, The Goons themselves have worn out a fair number of pen nibs and bruised a few typewriter keyboards with their own personal accounts. The problems only arise when one tries to piece it all together and produce one coherent picture.

For, despite all that has been said and written, there is a remarkable lack of consistency. Even The Goons have not always agreed on their individual roles, neither have they seen eye to eye on the part the shows played in the revolution of sound comedy. On top of this, outside attempts to rationalize their unique brand of humour have only served to cloud the issue.

The Story of The Goons attempts to explain how and why it started and the impact and effect The Goons had on British comedy. At the same time, it takes an in-depth look at the three men who made it possible.

Apart from the many sources gratefully acknowledged in the text, sincere thanks are extended to the following who helped to dot the I's and cross the T's.

His Royal Highness, The Prince of Wales, for permission to quote from his foreword to *More Goon Show Scripts*. Mr Peter Sellers for finding time during a very busy period of filming to talk about the Goon days. To Dennis Main Wilson who produced the very first Goon Show and has remained an addict ever since. Mr John Browell for his kind help in talking about his many years as producer of later shows. To Mr Theo Cowan who generously made available the collection of Mr Sellers' personal albums of cuttings. Mrs Sue Evans, Mr Sellers' secretary, for her unfailing co-operation. The Reverend Frederick Secombe for his invaluable help with stories about his younger brother Harry. Miss Norma Farnes, Mr Milligan's manager, for her assistance with background information on Spike.

Sincere thanks also to author Peter Evans for permission to quote from his life of Peter Sellers and for his personal recollections of their friendship. The same to Mr Herbert Kretzmer, song-writer and dramatic critic of the *Daily Express*. Mr Vincent Mulchrone of the *Daily Mail*, for permission to quote from his report on the last Goon Show and his behind-the-scenes account of the rehearsal. Mr James Thomas, television critic of the *Daily Express* for his help with material on the original show. Mr Con Mahoney, head of BBC Radio Light Entertainment.

The Author and Publisher wish to thank the following for permission to reproduce their photographs:

Section One

BBC Copyright Photographs.	Pages: 1, 2 top, 3 top, 3 bottom.
Syndication International.	Pages: 4 top, 4 bottom, 5, 6 bottom, 7, 8.
S & G Press Agency Ltd.	Page 2 bottom.
P.A. Photo.	Page 6 top.

Section Two

BBC Copyright Photographs.	Pages: 10, 16.
London Express.	Pages: 9, 11 bottom, 12 bottom, 13, 14 top.
Syndication International.	Pages: 11 top, 14 bottom.
S & G Press Agency Ltd.	Pages: 12 top, 15.

Section Three

Syndication International.	Pages: 18 top, 18 bottom, 20 bottom, 21, 22 top, 22 bottom, 23.
London Express.	Page 17.
Universal Pictorial Press.	Page 19.
P.A. Photo.	Page 20 top.
Keystone Press Agency Ltd.	Page 24.

Section Four

Syndication International.	Pages: 26 bottom left, 27 top right, 27 bottom right, 28 top, 32.
P.A. Photo.	Pages: 27 bottom left, 27 top left.
London Express.	Pages: 25, 31.
British Lion Films.	Page 26 top.
Rank Organisation Ltd.	Page 26 bottom right
S & G Press Agency Ltd.	Page 28 bottom.
Rex Features Ltd.	Page 29.
Associated Press Photo.	Page 30.

Acknowledgement

The still from 'Never Let Go' supplied by courtesy of The Rank Organisation Limited.

Chapter One

TREMOR OF A MIRTHQUAKE

It all began at the inauspicious hour of 6.45 p.m. on Monday, 28th May, 1951, when most people were still strap-hanging on their way home from work or too busy tucking into their dinner to switch on the radio. The curious handful that did heard the refined voice of an announcer intone, somewhat unnecessarily, 'This is the BBC Home Service.' His words were promptly followed by a fanfare of trumpets and a hideous cacophony of incomprehensible noises. The announcer asked the listeners, who were in no position to reply, 'What is the zaniest comedy show on the air today?'

The voice of a virtually unknown young writer-comic called Spike Milligan answered in sepulchral tones that would not have been out of place in a quiz for congenital idiots, 'Er – Today in Parliament?'

The announcer, exuding an enthusiasm that resembled a fight promoter introducing the main protagonists, retorted, 'No. It's those Crazy People, the Goons.'

And so was born a form of surrealistic, bubbling, off-beat humour that was to revolutionize sound comedy. In time, The Goons were to assume cult proportions and their voices and catchphrases would be repeated in factory canteens, offices, shops, boardrooms, messdecks and barracks throughout the English-speaking world. Royalty became addicts and invited them home; university dons, dockers, statesmen and film stars became devotees, while intellectuals read deep sociological and psychological significance into the pomposity-pricking charades that appealed to toddlers as well as veterans of countless Darby and Joan Clubs.

But there was little or no sign of the things to come after that first broadcast; the promised mirthquake had about as much effect on the seismograph of listener reaction as a damp squid. It had moments of outrageous hilarity, but the jokes and sketches seemed too way-out for audiences who saw the quick-fire patter of ITMA as the ultimate in aural entertainment. Milligan reflected ruefully, 'This brilliant rubbish is twenty years ahead of its time.' He was both right and wrong; the show *was* too avant-garde, in the way that Picasso's three-eyed women were when they first appeared, but it did not take anywhere near Spike's estimate of twenty years before it caught on. From a show ratings point of view the snowball of listeners became an avalanche in a fraction of the time he predicted.

It says a lot for the pyrotechnic brilliance of The Goons that the pioneer script, stamped RETAIN FOR ARCHIVES, can still set the ribs aching even when read and not heard. In fact, some of the more idiotic lines have been pencilled out; whether they were considered too far-fetched – 'At last. A programme for people without radio sets' – or whether the show was over-running no one can recall with accuracy after all these years. The time at which it was broadcast certainly doesn't indicate any great degree of confidence on the part of the programme planners.

The half hour show had actually been recorded the day before in the Aeolian Hall, a small sound studio sandwiched between art galleries and upper crust shops in exclusive Bond Street. The stage itself was cramped and snaked with cables and fronted with old-fashioned microphones that looked like miniature tennis rackets. A team of sound engineers were huddled over batteries of Grams wondering whether they could provide the till-then unheard-of special effects that the script demanded. Tapes were not in common use, and it meant a frenetic rush from one turntable to another to blend the noises.

At 10.30 a.m. four weird-looking men mounted the stage and began a read-through, and promptly broke the comedian's cardinal rule by laughing at their own jokes. They giggled, played pranks, and made last-minute alterations whenever they thought of something funnier or sillier. It would have been difficult to have found a more dissimilar bunch of men than Peter Sellers, Harry Secombe, Spike Milligan and

Michael Bentine. They sounded like the opening lines of a stag party joke: an India-born Irishman, a Watford-born Peruvian, a Jewish-Protestant, and a Welshman with a hysterical glass-breaking laugh. But they all had one thing in common: an outrageous sense of the idiotic and a burning ambition to crash through the barrier of conformist comedy that was shackling sound radio.

Sellers, the religious hybrid, was fast making a name for himself as a mimic and impersonator with a seemingly limitless repertoire; Bentine, the Eton and Sorbonne educated son of a South American scientist of international renown, was enjoying a reputation as an intellectual comic with a brand of humour that was marked for its originality (he could spell-bind an audience with just a chair as a prop); Harry Secombe, a bubbly, effervescent lad from Swansea with a slick music hall routine and a fine but untrained tenor voice; and Terence 'Spike' Milligan, a broody, melancholic man who had started as a musician then discovered a word-spinning talent that was capable of adding a new dimension to radio laughter-making.

All tended to have the same mop-headed hair style, as if collectively they had been hauled through a hawthorn hedge backwards. Milligan's emotional barometer fluctuated between agony and ecstasy; Secombe was already showing signs of Pickwickian overweight, while Sellers had a fondness for puffing out his cheeks and pulling faces that would have won a prize at a Cumbrian gurning* competition. Bentine's wire-wool black hair and beard were real, the Chester Conklin squint wasn't. It had required hours of practice before he could lock and hold his cross-eyes in position for the duration of his act.

At 5 p.m. the unsuspecting audience was admitted and treated to a 'warm-up' session that left them, to put it mildly, somewhat bewildered. Milligan put his coat on back to front, Sellers began talking into a wire-framed inspection lamp, Secombe picked up the producer one-handed, and every now and then someone dropped their trousers. If the mood took

* Face pulling competition.

them they held an impromptu jazz session with Sellers on the drums and Milligan playing the trumpet. Dennis Main Wilson, the young Producer who had been instrumental in them getting a break, confessed recently, 'I really couldn't control them. It was mad stuff for those days; absolutely brand new and totally unfettered by anyone else's style. They were completely complementary to each other.'

After the warm-up, the red lights flashed and the recording proper began. The audience could have been forgiven for believing there wasn't even the proverbial hairline separating genius from lunacy. The four men changed voices and characters with the rapidity of machine gun fire, and they were not quite ready for such imbecile lines as, 'So pull your chairs up to the ceiling; fill up your glasses with potassium cyanide and let The Goons do the rest.'

The apprehension and opposition of the BBC's hierarchy to the zany quartet ever getting air space seemed about to be justified. The show wasn't making sense. Looking back Dennis Main Wilson recalls the uphill fight for recognition. 'There was a handful of people, I was among them, who had great faith in their brand of comedy which for the first time created beautiful mind pictures. But people at the BBC were chary, and even when the show was agreed upon I was called in and told that an official directive had been issued stating that in no way could it be called The Goon Show. No one would know what it meant. It was insisted that we would call it "The Junior Crazy Gang starring those Crazy People – The Goons".' Later Main Wilson was able to get the secateurs to that tongue-twister and prune it to manageable size, but some executives, with judge-like remoteness still called them The Coons, as if they were some minstrel act, or the Go-Ons, which sounded like a dancing troupe.

Looking through the faded newspaper clippings of the period there is nothing to indicate what kind of impact The Goons's debut made; it seems to have been studiously ignored. The original script, however, although unwieldly and disjointed in parts, shows flashes of that brilliance that was to characterize the series in its heyday. One of its main faults was that it tried to pack in too many sketches instead of sticking to one main story line. But the alchemy for transmuting an everyday occurrence into eighteen-carat lunacy was already evident. Leafing through the original script one is transported back to a tip-up seat in the Aeolian Hall and, aided by memory, the voices live again.

Sellers: Here, next to me, standing on the head of the producer, is our author. We leave him to tell you his story. Mr Arnold Pringle.

Secombe: My name is Jones. I write this programme strictly for radio – but they said as a radio show, it was ahead of its time.

Sellers: When was that?

Secombe: 1852.

Sellers: Continue.

Secombe: I shall. I thought of many titles and finally settled on...

Milligan: Yuckabakaba.

Secombe: Every day I phoned the BBC in the hopes of contacting some influential person – I finally managed to get one of the heads – this I mounted on a pike.

Sellers: How jolly!

Secombe: Yes. At that time I was living in dire poverty – have you ever lived in dire poverty, friend?

Sellers: No, I have a little flat in Brockley.

Secombe: What a merry place to be sure – continuing my story – I was very, very poor ... worry turned me grey ... this gave me a peculiar appearance as I was completely bald at the time. As my last resource I opened up a little tobacconist's shop in Town. Unfortunately, the little tobacconist caught me. He sent for the police and so I...

The sweating sound effects men produced the courtroom noise of a pounding gavel and the rustle of legal documents; The Goons the background hub-bub. Secombe paid his fine 'with trembling fingers – but they wanted money'. And so he became a fugitive from justice pursued up the Great North

Road by a squad car at ninety miles an hour and only caught when his shoes wore out.

The audience were in stitches but still bemused: could The Goons maintain this reckless pace of non-stop humour? Still feeling their feet they didn't even try. They broke up the programme with musical interludes by Ray Ellington, a sepia-coloured singer with a gravel-pit voice, the Stargazers 'who appeared by courtesy of the Greenwich Observatory' and Max Geldray, a virtuoso harmonica player.

A skit on the BRM racing car typified the ability of The Goons to capitalize on topical subjects. Why BRM? 'Well, that's the sound it makes, sort of Brrrmmmm! Brrrmmmm!'

Sellers slipped into a perfect impersonation of Raymond Glendenning, the moustachioed doyen of sporting commentators. 'The International car races will soon be in full swing. In the past years the Italians have run away with all the prizes ... in some cases before the race had even started. But this year they will have to contend with Britain and the BRM.'

The programme was an amalgam of ideas, but Spike Milligan was mainly responsible for giving them cohesion, and what amazed the audience was the fact that The Goons found it every bit as amusing as they did. Bentine revelled in the role of a Grand Prix entrepreneur. 'Here's five thousand pounds, I want you to go to Italy and bring back the finest motoring brains that money can buy.'

Sellers sped off to a sound effects exit which permitted Bentine to comment, 'Three weeks later he arrived back with a glass jar. In it were the finest motoring brains that money could buy.'

It was a short sketch but with the aid of the sound effects The Goons were able to conjure up the 'mind pictures' which so impressed Dennis Main Wilson. The BRM met an ignominious end when it collapsed to the sound of rending metal and shattering glass as Lady Quilter christened it with champagne. Some people didn't take too kindly to the gentle satirizing of a much vaunted project, but over the years the public were to realize that nothing was sacred to The Goons.

They elevated micky-taking to a fine art. At the time of the first show 'Dick Barton, Special Agent' was a revered top-of-the-pops programme with young and old alike, almost a national institution in fact, but it didn't prevent The Goons doing a send-up which anyone less adventurous would have considered near sacrilege.

After the famous introductory music, Milligan announced, 'Dick Barton, Special Agent,' and Secombe took it up:

'In our last episode you will remember we left, Dick, Jock and Snowey trapped in a gas filled sewer (which you will remember, was beneath a haddock-stretching factory in Park Lane). You will remember they were suspended by their feet. (You will remember they *had* feet.) Jock works himself free and cuts Dick and Snowey down.'

Between them, Milligan, Secombe, Sellers and Bentine played the well-known characters with tongue-in-cheek hilarity although barely deviating from the fair-play, derring-do image of the originals, and they avoided the pitfall of being malicious.

It ended on an explosive note that had the audience rolling in the aisles.

Sellers (Barton): Look, they've thrown something through the door.

Secombe (Snowey): Great Scott! It's an atom bomb!

Milligan (Jock): What'll we do?

Sellers: Quick men, put your fingers in your ears.

TREMENDOUS EXPLOSION

'Listen again tomorrow to "Dick Barton's Special Funeral".'

This was followed by another musical interlude after which the announcer said, 'The next part of the programme follows as soon as it has been written.' There was a modicum of truth in the quip, for as Dennis Main Wilson recalled more than twenty years later, 'There was a fair amount of ad-libbing going on, plus a lot of comic antics which had the audience in stitches but confused the listeners at home because they couldn't see what was happening.'

By now that first night audience had begun to realize that they were really witnessing something unique in entertain-

15

ment; weaned on traditional comedy they sensed that here at last was a major breakthrough. In some seemingly miraculous way the four men on the stage seemed to *become* the loony characters they portrayed, and with superb sound effects conjured up a situation that was real and yet not real. To the exotic strains of Eastern music the saga 'The Quest for Tutankhamen' was introduced with Sellers playing the intrepid explorer Sir Harold Porridge.

'For months my expedition has been digging for the lost tomb of the greatest of the Pharaohs, King Tutankhamen, two thousand Khurdish coolies and their wives, 500 Besarabian porters and their bags, and 600 dromedaries, all engaged in the task of excavating. For two years we dug every inch of ground – then *finally* – we received a cable from the Egyptian Government. It said simply...'

Secombe: 'Stop digging Hackney Marshes – try Egypt.'

It was vintage Goonery; taking a straight situation and carrying it to its illogical conclusion. A commonplace phrase was stood on its head to provoke ripples of mirth.

Milligan (playing a co-explorer): It was a hot night in June. Unable to sleep I took out a sleeping pill. I then woke it up and swallowed it. In the deep slumber that followed I heard a sepulchral voice that said...

Bentine (on echo): Go to the Valley of Kings. There you will find the tomb of Tutankhamen!

Milligan: But how do I get in?

Bentine: Tut-and-Kham-in!

And so the expedition sailed, pills were issued for the dread lurgi, the sound effects team provided a background of seagulls, pounding waves and howling winds. Naturally it was a trip beset by perils.

Secombe: There's a fire in Number One Hold, captain.

Sellers: Oh! I'll come down right away. This cabin's freezing.

Announcer: Two months' grim sailing and then from the crow's nest the news they had all waited for.

Milligan: Der-land ahead.

Bentine: How far?

Milligan: Oh! – ummmmmmm-der-lemme see now-err-no prompting from the crew now – 4, 6, 5, 7 der-well I should say...

Sound SHIP HITTING LAND

Milligan: Der – mind if I go ashore?

Spike's near-incoherent babbling was an early milestone, for it introduced a character that was to become a Milligan masterpiece – Eccles, the part time human being who spent eighteen years of his infanthood in kindergarten.

The quest ended with the eventual discovery of the tomb and the shattering denouement that it had all been in vain: The King was dead.

The final item was a gentle leg-pull at the expense of the Festival of Britain which was launched to give the world an image of a resurgent 'with it' nation rising Phoenix-like after the war years of austerity and hardship. Called 'Salute to Britain' it merits a nostalgic mention for Secombe sang – in the bath.

The part of his wife was to have been played by an actress, but she was off sick so Sellers took over.

Sellers: You in the barf, Fred?

Secombe: Yarst. Why?

Sellers: Well, I want to clean your boots.

Secombe: Oh! Blimey! Now I'll have to take 'em orf.

The strains of Land of Hope and Glory echoed through the Aeolian Hall and Bentine in statesmanlike tones boomed, 'Today the Mother-Land can still raise her proud face to the skies and say...'

Secombe: HEELLLPPPP!!!

The show was over. The audience filed into Bond Street with mixed feelings. Like most people who experience something unique, they were reluctant to express an opinion for fear of being hopelessly wrong. They had laughed fit to burst, but could that crazy kind of humour be maintained? There was also a sneaking suspicion in their minds that the four comic 'geniuses' would all end up round the bend before it took a hold on the public imagination.

In his office high up in the BBC's Television Centre, Dennis

Main Wilson recently reflected on his own views after that opening night. 'It was slow to catch on. But having experienced the hard fight to even get it on the air we were not all that much surprised. It was years ahead of its time and a bit too hairy for Aunti Beeb. For three years the BBC had rejected the idea of a Goon Show, so we couldn't expect the public to accept it over night. But we were confident we could make it. We did, but it was mainly by word of mouth; people talked about The Goons in the pubs, at work and in clubs. There were thirteen programmes in the first series, and twenty-five in the second, by which time it had been retitled The Goon Show and they were quite famous.'

As Wilson looted his memory bank he recalled that Secombe's first song was almost his last. 'Michael Standing, the then Head of Variety and a charming man, called me into his office and said, "Your friend Secombe sings out of tune. We must have no more of it." I stalled and assured Michael that Harry would get better. When Harry sang again I was called in and had my balls torn off. It would appear, he said, that the BBC was standing in the way of my production and if it was all right with me the BBC proposed to go its own way while I could go mine.'

The hint was taken and Secombe did not sing the following week, but The Goons overcame the problem with a not-too-cunning ploy. A special script was written around a court scene in which Harry was in the dock and Bentine was prosecuting counsel. The cross examination, 'Tell me, Secombe, what makes you sing,' was carried out to music from Carmen and Harry's robust tenor replied with Covent Garden mellowness. (Harry later took lessons from the famous Italian singing master Manlio di Veroli and with his virtually rebuilt voice could have earned a living in serious opera.)

After the first recording Wilson went off to edit the script; ironically his biggest cuts were in that commodity of which no comic can get enough – laughter. The dilemma facing him was that people at home would wonder what the hell was going on if he left in all the gusts of laughter. They wouldn't be able to *hear* anything funny and wouldn't appreciate the audience were just chuckling at the unscripted antics of the four men. It was a problem that was to dog later producers when they took over the show; but there was no way of curbing the on-stage antics for it was the only way The Goons could work.

An early protest appeared in the magazine *Woman*: 'Goonery is all very well visually, but I wish the brilliant nit wits in The Goon Show would remember that they are playing to a sound radio audience, not TV. One very wet Sunday night I sat at a rehearsal of their programme in London, and laughed myself silly at their antics. But when I listened to the broadcast later, so much that was funny in the studio just didn't come over the air.'

It was a valid criticism, but as Dennis Main Wilson had discovered, 'There was no way of controlling them.' They were still at it in 1954, by which time Bentine had left the team, and Jonah Barrington, the distinguished critic of the *Daily Sketch*, urged them to 'Simmer Down Goons'. The particular programme had dealt with an attempt by special agent Ned Seagoon to thwart Hungaria's football supremacy by putting dynamite in the toes of their boots. 'The pandemonium was terrific, and audience laughter clouded many finer points in a brilliant script. But, even so, it was obvious that this, the first of a new Goon series was the fastest, nuttiest, most zany, screwball, crack-brained and bug house production yet turned out by the team of Sellers, Secombe and Milligan.' Then came the warning, 'But if they want to stay tops – if they want to jump the last hurdle between the "up and coming" and the "big time class" – then I must counsel caution ... too much pace can ruin everything.'

There was no compromise from The Goons. Milligan's attitude was simple: if listeners didn't have the nimble wit to follow them they must do the other thing. He totally rejected Barrington's advice to adopt the old wartime navy dictum, 'The speed of the convoy is governed by the slowest ship'. And Milligan was right, the public learned to keep up with The Goons. As they were prepared to drop everything rather than miss the show, so they came to regard it as a point of honour not to miss a gag. No one likes to admit being slow-witted. Anyway, there was always a ready market for those inexplicable gales of laughter which were edited out – they were given to shows which were a bit short on the mirth stakes.

Although they worked well together, Bentine and Milligan did not always see eye to eye with each other, and a parting was inevitable; it was the old story of the irresistible force and the immovable object. There was no acrimony when Bentine left comparatively early to plough his own furrow. 'I was,' he confessed later, 'always a breakaway Goon with an urge to apply my logical nonsense as opposed to their nonsensical logic.'

Sellers and Milligan, diametrically opposed in so many ways, set out to create a fantasy world where the characters were not just voices coming out of a radio set, but *real*, live, breathing people who trespassed into the sitting rooms of an audience which now numbered millions. And so they built up that galaxy of impossible characters who were so brilliantly drawn that they assumed positive identities in the eyes of the fans. Sometimes the voices came first, sometimes the names. Milligan and Sellers drew on their experiences of life in India to create the ghastly but lovable bounder Major Dennis Bloodnok, a seedy, bemedalled coward from the Rajputana Rifles. Bluebottle came from a particularly obnoxious child Sellers recalled from his schooldays. Spike drew on Dickens for Henry Crun, a stooping Victorian relic with a huge adam's apple perched above a wing collar and hands as gnarled as walnuts. There was pea-brained Eccles; the velvet-voiced Hercules Gryptype-Thynne, cad and arch villain, whom many thought sounded remarkably like George Sanders; Count 'Jim' Moriarty, the con-man in an astrakhan coat; and Miss Minnie Bannister, who lived in a bungalow with hundreds of steps to the first floor. William 'Mate' Cobblers is alleged to be alive and posing as a timber expert with an uncanny sense of touch that enables him to pronounce a piece of wood as solid without the slightest hesitation. Neddy Seagoon and the leek-chewing Ned of Wales, are of course the giggling flesh and blood Secombe.

It is no exaggeration or extravagant claim to say that no set of characters have enjoyed such widespread acclaim or affection.

Sellers explained their lasting popularity this way: 'The public identified themselves with these characters and situations because to many of them they were more than just funny voices. They were caricatures of real people.'

It's not as simple as that for Milligan, a tortured genius with a massive social chip on his slumped shoulders. When asked to analyse the humour that took such a grip on the nation he said, 'Essentially it is critical comedy. It is against bureaucracy, and on the side of human beings. Its starting point is one man shouting gibberish in the face of authority, and proving by fabricated insanity that nothing could be as mad as what passes for ordinary living.'

It is probably as near to an accurate assessment as one will ever get. Too many attempts have been made to dissect the show, and too many differing interpretations presented for anyone to be really sure. Names like Lewis Carroll, Edward Lear, James Joyce, Ionesco, Dylan Thomas, Thurber, and so on, have been bandied around to try and trace the origin of the humour, but all have been unsuccessful. The Goons are not a one man product; they are the work of an inimitable team. And most people are content to accept that and just lean back and enjoy them.

Dennis Main Wilson, when recalling those early days, echoed Milligan's thoughts. 'Spike was born in India of a military family, and so he grew up with an inbuilt hatred of the Establishment. That kind often end up creating their own establishments, and that's what he has done.'

That may explain why, even when The Goons were enjoying an unparallelled following, the BBC was still antagonistic. What had become as much a part of living to the average man and woman as the crossword, the weekly wash, the Sunday joint and Saturday round of golf was still a thorn in the flesh to a handful of backward-looking officials cocooned from the march of time in their admin aeries. Peter Eton, who took over from Dennis Main Wilson and produced it for five and a half years, expressed his frustration in an introduction to *The Book of The Goons*:

'The difficulties inherent in working with such talent and over such long periods made my life an exciting trial, though the bumbling bureaucracy of the BBC presented me with far more problems than The Goons themselves. Altogether I logged thirty attempts by them to stop the show. For instance, one week Major Bloodnok was awarded the OBE for emptying dustbins during the heat of battle – just after two BBC executives had received the honour. I was called up and warned about committing further breaches of taste. On another occasion Peter (Sellers) imitated the Queen's voice during the hilarious launching of an attempt to dislodge the pigeons from Trafalgar Square, and I was hauled up again. The officials threatened to take the show off altogether in the face of this further example of "rank bad taste". I believe that it was only John Snagge's continued defence of the programme and insistence on Spike's right to freedom as a writer, which saved us.'

Fortunately for the listening and viewing public the Wilsons, Etons, Milligans and Snagges have always had the talent and integrity to refuse to be steamrollered into mute acceptance of the 'safe' and 'uncontroversial'.

Ironically those who were scared stiff that the honours system would be brought into disrepute and Royalty offended by *lese majeste* had to eat humble pie in the long run: Sellers and Secombe were both honoured, and all three have been invited to informal dinners with the Royal Family.

Today the only active campaign comes from those who want a return of The Goons, but whether or not that will happen only The Goons themselves can answer. This study makes no presumptions to crystal-gazing on the subject of where it will all end, but it can trace the tangled skein back to where it all began.

Chapter Two

TAVERN IN THE TOWN

Anyone who has met The Goons has expressed amazement at how people as different as chalk from cheese, with totally alien backgrounds and upbringing, could form such a perfect team. But as someone shrewdly observed they can be compared to the tributaries of a great river which can have different sources and paths but are destined to meet in the end. Ignoring the geographical analogy, there is some indefinable chemistry that brings about great partnerships: Rolls *had* to meet Royce, Laurel–Hardy, Morecambe–Wise, Rodgers–Hart, Gilbert–Sullivan, Groucho–Harpo–Chico.

The point of fusion for The Goons couldn't, however, have been less glamorous or more unromantic: The Grafton Arms, a Victorian pub in a narrow Victoria street lined with coster-barrows and sharp-eyed shoppers wanting value for money. The scars of war were still visible in London, there were huge timber-blackened gaps where houses had once stood, demob suits hadn't yet worn out, and there were utility labels on a vast range of goods. Men faced with the prospect of earning a living were missing the camaraderie of the services, and any excuse served for a get-together. But generally there was a mood of buoyant optimism abroad. The war had been won and the Welfare State was just around the corner with its promises of a land fit for heroes. True, there was still rationing: the weekly joint could sit almost unnoticed in the palm of your hand and bananas were as rare as radium; but the street lights were on again, and the last of the evacuees was home and settled, and Vera Lynn's bluebirds were back at Dover.

The tavern was run by Jimmy Grafton, an ex-Major who had won the Military Cross at the Battle of Arnhem and who, in between pulling pints, wrote extremely good comedy scripts. Somehow or other it became a meeting place for aspiring actors, producers, comics and writers who, glad to be back in civvy street, were bubbling with new and adventurous ideas.

Secombe's and Milligan's stars had already crossed in the heat of battle in the Western Desert. It was an explosive introduction that could have come straight out of a Goon show. The campaign against Rommel was at its peak and myopic Lance Bombardier 924378 Secombe, his steel-frame army issue glasses held together by adhesive tape, was hunched over a transmitter in a wireless truck. On a hill-top high above, the artillery had dug-in a battery of heavy 7.2 howitzers. With drumbeat regularity they gave out ear-shattering roars. Suddenly there was a terrible sound like a miniature avalanche followed by the rending of metal. Secombe peeped out and saw a wrecked gun a few feet from his truck. 'The bastards are throwing their guns at us now,' he roared indignantly.

But it wasn't the Hun, it was his own side wreaking the havoc. For a shadowy figure carrying a hurricane lamp suddenly emerged from the gloom to ask plaintively, 'Anybody seen my gun? I had it a few minutes ago.' As the lamp illuminated the well-and-truly-spiked howitzer the melancholy-loaded voice said, 'Can I have it back?'

The dishevelled figure in a rumpled battle dress introduced himself; he was, he explained apologetically, Gunner Milligan, 954024, of the Royal Regiment of Artillery. The gun's crew, in their haste to clobber the Hun, hadn't taken the elementary precaution of securing the gun, so that when the firing lanyard had been jerked the recoil had sent it plunging helter-skelter down the 150-foot high wadi. There is no record of what happened to the gun, but the meeting marked the beginning of a long and lasting friendship between the two men. (The story has been embellished and polished over the years and the versions differ in detail according to who is telling it – Harry or Spike – but it is true for all that.)

Later, when the combined efforts of Secombe and Milligan had contributed to the downfall of Hitler they worked together in a number of forces shows, and when the war ended they still kept in touch. Looking at Harry now it is hard to believe that he and the bean-pole Milligan once shared their limited wardrobes.

Sellers, demobbed from the RAF, was taking work where and when he could find it. Bentine, the former Air Force Intelligence Officer, was carving a niche for himself as a wild-eyed comic with an egg-head approach to humour. When Secombe met them he discovered they all shared common ideas on the future path that comedy should tread. He couldn't wait to introduce them to Spike. 'You'll like him. He's one of us,' but he added cautiously, 'I must warn you, he's quite mad.'

And so the quartet began to meet in Jimmy Grafton's hostelry and talk over their ideas with animated enthusiasm. It was an ideal rendezvous for hard up entertainers for Jimmy was literally mine host; he often provided the beer free. At the time Spike was living in an attic room above the pub and doing odd jobs to make both ends meet. The garret-like existence seemed to suit Milligan who slept in a sleeping bag below a portrait of Franz Kafka, and spent his spare time hammering out scripts with two fingers on an ancient typewriter that would have fetched a fortune at a Sotheby auction. He was promptly dubbed 'The Prisoner of Zenda'.

Grafton encouraged them to give impromptu concerts for his customers in an upstairs room, and as the reputation of the 'pub performers' spread, people like Margaret Lockwood, Ronald Searle and Dennis Main Wilson began to drop in. A small item by show-biz writer Bill Boorne announced the formation of The Goon Club, but it passed almost unnoticed. A few shoulders were shrugged indifferently and there were one or two murmurs of, 'So what?'

Mr Boorne's write-up indicates the vagueness of the project. 'Four young men' – he wrote – 'are planning to form a new "crazy gang" when they have made even bigger names for themselves as single acts.

'Already they have formed themselves into what they call The Goon Club and meet regularly at a pub in Victoria, with a strange ritual and a handshake all their own. Soon they will have a club badge – a humanized peanut.' (Alongside was a line drawing of a hair-spouting peanut with a pair of eyes that looked like poached eggs.)

The Goons were listed as: Bentine ('allowed to go into the wilderness because the "brains" of the theatre business thought his act was too crazy'), Alfred Marks, Harry Secombe and Peter Sellers. Milligan was dismissed as 'also being interested'.

Grafton, known as KOGVOS – King of the Goons and the Voice of Sanity – encouraged Bentine, Sellers, Milligan and Secombe to record a couple of the shows which kept his customers in stitches. By then Spike had moved into the Sellers household at 211b High Road, East Finchley, but he retained his monastic aloofness, sleeping on the kitchen floor and restricting his personal possessions to a level that would have made a hermit feel affluent and pampered.

Bentine and Milligan were helped with the script by Larry Stephens, a young thriller-writer who had turned to comedy. The enthusiasm of those upstairs pub audiences was not shared by the British Broadcasting Corporation which made polite noises when the recording was played, then promptly forgot it. Looking back, Dennis Main Wilson recalls, 'The BBC consistently turned it down for three years, then Pat Dixon, a producer, listened to it and was impressed but not optimistic. "It's too far out," he warned, but he submitted it and it was agreed to give the show a trial.'

Odd paragraphs about the pending show appeared in inconspicuous corners of the newspapers and people began to ask, 'Who and what the hell are The Goons?'

James Thomas, the radio critic for the *News Chronicle*, then very much alive and kicking, sat at his typewriter and tried to shed light into dark places with an article which began 'What is a Goon?'

'A Goon is someone with a one-cell brain. Anything that is not basically simple puzzles a Goon. His language is inarticulate; he thinks in the fourth dimension.'

Milligan was quoted as saying, 'We pride ourselves that since the days of the swamps, Goons have not moved (intellectually) one inch.'

26

(Milligan had in fact borrowed the name from the *Daily Mirror* Popeye cartoon in which a horde of weird monsters who spoke in scribbles had invaded a desert island.)

Thomas hinted at the teething troubles the show had experienced when he revealed that three producers had walked out before Dennis Main Wilson had stuck his neck out and agreed to do it. 'Goon humour is obviously crazy – and clever. It will either be loved or detested,' said Thomas, hedging his bet.

Wilson knew there was no magic recipe for overnight success and he realized there was a long uphill haul ahead, but he was never in any doubt about the final outcome. A decade later, with a string of television hits tucked under his belt including the formation of the George Mitchell Glee Club and the production of 'Hancock's Half Hour' and 'Till Death Do Us Part' plus many other pioneer projects, he recalled: 'Once every too few years you get a show where everything gels. The cast is right, the script is good and the producer happy. The Goons had a God-given, or whatever you care to call it, gift. It's something you're born with. You just can't define it, if you could you'd end up with as many Goons as there are civil servants. Anyway, the result was a form of pure comedy that will never date.'

James Thomas, who would have given his eye teeth to have been sitting with the BBC's governors when the first recording went out – they had committed themselves to a cautious 'it's a rather extravagant form of humour' – was one of the first to rhapsodize. He wrote, 'When it comes to comic adventures, radio must win hands down over TV.' Sacred cows went tumbling down like skittles in an alley, Establishment figures were lampooned, the props of society given a good shaking, and ivory towers stormed with total irreverence; and the listening public lapped it up like thirsty desert travellers arriving at an unexpected oasis.

Even when the show caught on, The Goons continued to work and rehearse in an upstairs room of The Grafton Arms, where KOGVOS Jimmy exercised a restraining influence and saw to it that while they pushed comedy to the brink

27

they didn't topple it over the edge like Milligan's cannon. It became voguish to be a member of the privileged audience in that cluttered smoke-filled room and even *Picture Post*, a magazine that tended to be a bit toffee-nosed and assign its writers and cameramen to world shattering events of moment, found itself visiting The Grafton Arms and doing a centre page spread on the four young men who specialized in comedy 'that doesn't despise your intelligence'.

Bentine was soon to depart after that. Spike and Mike had been on a collision course for some time, and sooner or later the crunch had to come. While Milligan aspired towards perfection Bentine seemed to have achieved it. There seemed nothing he didn't know or couldn't do. Sellers recalled, 'Spike resented the fact that there was no area in which Bentine was not the master, despite the fact that he was a near-genius himself.'

In fairness, the amiable envy was shared by the other Goons who had not had the advantages of Bentine's education; he could speak five languages and had graduated in nuclear physics. Time after time they had tried to up-stage him but invariably met with failure. When they all went to Sherwood Forest they presented him with a long bow and Bentine promptly relegated Robin Hood to the role of another also ran. When they went to a RAF station for a special show and heard that the Polish adjutant was a master fencer, they immediately foresaw the cum-uppance of Bentine who had once confessed to dabbling with the epee and sabre. They contrived for a duel to take place in the gym and watched with dismay as Bentine routed the master.

When it came to Yoga, Bentine again displayed his supremacy by spending the whole of a train journey standing on his head while carrying out an erudite conversation with the other passengers in the carriage.

Milligan is a warm, compassionate, generous man who is not envious in a materialistic way, but he is terribly insecure and as a result dislikes being outshone. Apart from that he had very fixed ideas about the Goon scripts, which didn't run parallel to Bentine's. As far as he was concerned there was only room for one jockey on the horse.

The explanation for Michael's departure was that he was 'reading Dickens under the unlikely pseudonym of Emlyn Williams'. But even with his departure, Bentine retained a nostalgic affection for his old comrades and still speaks enthusiastically of the old Goon days. One of his favourite anecdotes perfectly illustrates how they were just as crazy off stage as they were on it. 'You could call it The Day The Goons Hoaxed a Nation', he said. It began in Grafton's office, where The Goons were having a routine script discussion. There was a briefcase on the table and the conversation turned to the large number of important documents left in buses, tubes and restaurants by top scientists and Civil Servants. 'Maybe we all had the idea together, or maybe it was Peter's ad-libbing the character of a Whitehall official muttering at the discovery of the briefcase full of vital documents in a phone box, but soon we were busy formulating the Plan. We wrote out a wonderful formula, full of long scientific words, calculations and equations, and covering two foolscap pages in small, close-set writing. Scrapings from a watch face to make a radioactive substance was mixed with peanut butter and put in a tube. Into another tube – we got them from a boy's chemistry set – we put cigar ash which looked reasonably like uranium. We left the case in a telephone kiosk at Victoria Station. Of course it was found and next day the papers were full of it.'

The top secret find was rushed to the Yard's forensic laboratory and there the saga ended in stony silence. Added Bentine, 'It would have been enlightening to see the lab boys' faces when they finally broke down the formula. Actually it was a recipe for making a good cup of tea!'

It is an enlightening story, for it not only shows how The Goons carried their crazy antics into their social life but it contains the key to their comedy and its success. Almost every sketch was originally taken from life. The wizardry came from illogical rationalizing. If you could climb Everest from the outside you could do it from the inside. The story of the Bristol Brabazon aeroplane led naturally to the Bristol

Brabagoon. If there was a North and South Pole it was obvious there had to be an East and West. When a newspaper reported that Westminster Pier was gradually sinking into the Thames mud and that someone had waded out and nailed an 'out of action' notice on the superstructure, it was inevitable that a programme would be built around it. When the QE2 was launched it provided the idea for a story 'The Building of the Goonitania', an 84,000 ton super liner, and the problems involved in getting it out of its bottle.

The four ex-service men had first teamed up after their demob in 1946. 'We wanted,' said Bentine, 'to do the Goon Shows then, but it was to take four years of hard work before it got off the ground.'

Attempts have been made to pretend there was a flaming row when Michael left; there wasn't. As Bentine explained, 'I was with The Goon Show till 1952, so the six years from 1946 till then represents a large chunk of my life. I remember we suffered enormous tensions in putting the shows together, but there was also the joyous side and the memories all four of us have. My relationship with Harry, Peter and Spike, which developed over those years, is an intensely personal one, and we found a friendship that is for ever. I had a large part in creating The Goon Shows, which have become a cult. If they are not of historical interest they are certainly of hysterical value. It was only reluctantly that I left the Show, for the reasons I stated in my book.'

In his autobiography *The Long Banana Skin*, published by Wolfe Publishing Ltd., Bentine has this to say about those pioneer days which began at The Grafton Arms public house in Victoria: 'Having our operations in a lovely old pub had its advantages. We were soon joined by the youthful and then-plump Peter Sellers, and the idea of welding ourselves together in a radically different comedy format slowly emerged. Peter had come into our orbit through the Windmill and at first had only seemed to be an excellent impressionist with a great talent for character voices. As our mutual friendship ripened we all began to see the possibilities which could arise from becoming a close-knit team.'

Encouraged by Jimmy Grafton and with the backing of BBC Producer Pat Dixon The Goon Show was launched.

'At first the anarchic humour that we specialized in drew only a small but devoted audience of afficionados and a trickle of somewhat weird fan mail.'

While Bentine was working in America he received a 'come home' plea from Milligan and Sellers asking him to join in the new Goon Show series. Another comedian, Graham Stark, had joined the show. 'Although he was a good performer I couldn't quite understand how this fitted in with the original idea and felt that the series must be well established, indeed, to make such a radical departure from our original conception of just the four of us.... I knew, intuitively, that The Goons would really get off the ground in a big way, if there were only three of them and, as I, at that time, with the exception of Spike, was the only self-contained writer-performer unit, I felt the choice of the one to leave must be me. The conviction grew on me, until I told Harry what I felt, to get his reaction. He was very upset, but he did see my point.'

Milligan and Sellers were also sad at the break-up. But stories appeared in the newspapers that there had been a row.

'This, understandably, upset Spike even more and the situation became very unhappy – after all, I was the one who, in my innocence, was doing the "Captain Oates" bit. Thank heavens, we can all laugh about it now, but in those days, we were more impressionable.'

A few months later Bentine made a special appearance on the show to disprove the feud stories.

'The contribution I made to The Goons was in real terms; firstly, the publicity I received with my second Hippodrome season was national and helped a lot to get us on the air. Secondly, creatively, I supplied a lot of ideas and lastly, I offered a broad range of characters.'

Looking back, it is amazing how The Goons not only managed to maintain an incredibly high standard but also got better and better. At the beginning of September 1954 they were back with a new series and every critic waited with pen poised for a sign of staleness, but 'The Starlings' was Goonery at its unbeatable best. Again they chose a serious environmental problem, turned it topsy turvy, yet managed to emerge with a script that had a lot of social significance. In an attempt to dislodge the birds from Trafalgar Square, 'The Ministry of Grit, Filth and Exportable Heads' launched 'Operation Cacophony' with the Brigade of Guards keeping up a non-stop barrage of noise which theoretically would make the decibel-sensitive birds fly off to less unpleasant climes. But of course the starlings stayed put. Landmarks like St Martin's in the Fields were destroyed by 'explodable lime', while the bird population continued to thrive, but the bureaucrats were not deterred; the solution was simple, destroy, rebuild, destroy, rebuild.

The programme epitomized Milligan's definition of his own work, yet what seemed so effortless was imposing a tremendous strain on him. The Goon Show was to become a Frankenstein's monster for the introspective perfectionist. But as yet there was no sign of the mental crack-up that was to come. The Goons went from series to series with their followers increasing in number all the time. In September 1954 they notched up the 100th Goon Show and everyone envisaged that like Methuselah it would go on for ever. How could anything end that had such a devoted following that even The Goon Show Preservation Society was formed?

When The Goons went in for songwriting the 'Ying Tong Song' made the charts – it repeated the process when it was re-issued seventeen years later. 'I'm walking Backwards for Christmas' sold 100,000 copies.

Off stage The Goons talked to each other in their own special brand of gobble-de-gook and used their stage names in preference to their own when they socialized. They did the same with their correspondence, no matter which part of the world they found themselves. The GPO was kept busy delivering a flood of telegrams, postcards and business letters from Henry Crun, Moriarty, Ned Seagoon, Eccles, Bluebottle and Gryptype Thynne. Those that weren't sealed in an envelope must have made the postman wonder in the interests of public safety whether the senders shouldn't be certified. Typical was a postcard from Sellers who was in America, to Milligan. 'Dear Eccles – No sign of Moriarty or Gryptype Thynne. Money running low, so low I've got to stoop down and pick it up as it goes by.'

During one show a joke misfired and brought near pandemonium. In inch high headlines the *Daily Mirror* proclaimed *Goon Show's Flying Saucer Shook the Listeners*. Below Clifford Davis wrote, 'Three times within a few minutes last night the BBC announced that flying saucers had been seen in the sky...

'Startled listeners to the Home programme's "Goon Show" rushed to their telephones to find out what was going on. The BBC switchboard was jammed with callers.

' "Sorry," the BBC told them, "it was all part of the show – JUST A JOKE."

'The interruptions by announcer Wallace Greenslade were dramatic and lifelike. "The Goon Show" had only just started when it was faded out. Announcer Greenslade said in his best BBC manner: "We must apologize for interrupting the programme, but a mysterious light has been seen over East Acton. If anyone can identify the object will they please phone the Defence Board – Milthorpe 0203." '

A few seconds later the show was again faded out and the announcement repeated. It happened a third time with a further statement that the object was heading for the North Pole and every effort was being made to contact the United Nations weather base there. Some people actually claimed to have seen the weird object, while others tried desperately to ring the non-existent Milthorpe number.

Wrote Davis, 'But for fifteen minutes the BBC had hoaxed millions of listeners. The BBC said after the broadcast, "Unfortunately a number of people took the interruptions seriously. We apologized to them when they phoned and pointed out that it was announced in the *Radio Times* that the programme was a recording." '

It revealed the hold The Goons had taken on the public's imagination and how they could make people genuinely believe their lunacy was real. For that matter, The Goons themselves had been carried away by their own brain children. They bought a sledge used by John Mills in his film 'Scott of the Antarctic', loaded it with bric-a-brac, a stuffed parrot, and a live dog; and topped with a Union Jack fluttering limply in the non-existent breeze, hand-hauled it through the West End. As it was summer and snow was at a premium, they tore off strips of paper and scattered it like confetti. During another escapade they donned Dawn Patrol leather helmets, ankle-length coats and flying goggles, and drove a battered Austin convertible through the peak-hour crowded streets at a breakneck walking pace. All the time they shouted lines associated with their favourite creations. A psychologist might find something of deep significance in their refusal to leave the fictional characters in the studio, but the public simply saw it as an excess of exuberance, rather like those distant days when couples danced the Charleston on the roofs of London taxis.

When Sellers, never a man to be interested in money for its own sake, was pressed to pay bills, he sent a stereotyped reply saying he had a simple routine where creditors were concerned – he put all their names in a hat and when he was flush he drew one out. Over-persistent people were warned that their names would not go in next time if they continued their harassment.

Sellers and Secombe loved every mad minute, but the strain was beginning to tell on Milligan with his unattainable quest for perfection. What at first seems hilariously funny assumes overtones of tragedy and sadness at second glance, as when Spike wanted to know what a sockful of cold custard sounded like when bashed against something. He solemnly went into the canteen at the Camden Theatre where many of the shows were recorded and asked the cook to make him a custard. The woman thinking he wasn't feeling well, did so. Milligan thanked her profusely, then took off his sock and poured the gooey mess into it, swung it round his head and walloped the wall. Then he shook his head sadly; it wasn't the effect he desired.

When he wanted the implausible tick of an atom bomb he would stand head cocked to one side urging the sound effects man to improve on it. 'It's not loud enough. Louder, go on, till it gets to feedback point.'

Perfection is unattainable, like trying to pin down a blob of mercury with the ball of the thumb. But Milligan could not accept that, any more than Michelangelo could when he struck his statue of Moses with a mallet and commanded it to speak. All the sculptor achieved was a crack in the statue and a massive dent in his pride. Similarly, Milligan could not call a halt to those self-inflicted wounds.

Sellers was also a perfectionist, but he was more resilient and funnelled his frustrations into other outlets. His obsession for buying gadgets and changing cars with the frequency that other men change their socks and underwear was simply an extension of his own personal quest for perfection. To date he has had more than one hundred cars ranging from a Rolls to a Mini. Each has been perfect in one or two details, but never wholly so. That's why he'll remain the car salesman's best customer. Sellers knows full well the car of his pipe-dreams has never left the drawing board and never will, but the quest for it is an ideal safety valve for his frustrations.

Secombe was the only member of the trio who didn't seem to suffer any hang-ups. He could take the rough and the smooth with equal aplomb. 'My stage image,' he confessed, 'is an extension of my private self. It's a job for show-offs, and I'm something of an extrovert and exhibitionist. I have no schizophrenic tendencies. I'm not a serious person and I'm able to convey a sense of fun because I really believe in it. This business about a clown being miserable deep down has never made sense to me.'

In his early days as a stand-up comic he died the death at the Grand Theatre, Bolton, during Wakes Week. Most of the time his act was greeted with stony silence and what applause there was was confined to the slow handclap variety. He was promptly fired and told to get the next train. Secombe took it in his stride. He cabled Bentine: 'Audience with me all the way Stop Managed to shake them off at

35

station.' Secombe would often be down but never, never out; he would always bounce back without a bruise.

As the popularity of The Goons grew, there were demands for them to make public appearances in music halls throughout the country and it was during one such personal appearance that the terrifyingly destructive effect the non-stop writing of Goon scripts was having on Milligan first emerged.

Chapter Three

DEATH IN COVENTRY

In the days before the bottom fell out of the car market, Coventry was a boom town where the workers took home fat pay packets and had plenty to spend on entertainment. So when The Goons during their round of music halls were booked for the Hippodrome, they looked forward to a lucrative engagement. Strictly speaking they were not billed as The Goons, but they were together and that was good enough for the public.

Milligan was a little more withdrawn than usual, and Sellers and Secombe recognized that he was going through a grey patch, but they were confident he could cope. Sellers had had previous experience of Spike suddenly blowing his top in a fit of seemingly uncontrollable fury, then almost instantly reverting to normality. He had seen Spike, when he was living at Peg Sellers' home, rush out on to the roof and loose a fusillade of blank shots from an antique pistol at some workmen who were disturbing his concentration. But Spike had been blown up twice in the war so he was entitled to a little eccentricity. Furthermore, he had been flogging himself turning out The Goon Show scripts, but he was too professional to take his personal problems on stage. They were wrong. The Hippodrome engagement was to end disastrously.

The Goon-style humour did not readily transfer to the flesh and blood stage, and the packed audience could hardly have

36

been described as ecstatic – chilly would have been an under-statement. When Milligan, Secombe and Sellers appeared as acrobats in a skit called 'Les Trois Charleys' it went like a lead balloon.

As Sellers recalls, 'The trouble was that audiences – and managers – were not all educated in Goon humour. They didn't always know when we were gagging and when we were serious.'

But audiences pay at the box office with hard cash, and if they don't like or don't understand something, they are per-fectly entitled to show their displeasure. Those Coventry folk were no exception. Spike in his intellectual arrogance couldn't go along with that and strongly objected to an-tagonism. During the show he did a comedy routine that ended with a trumpet solo that was greeted with cat-calls, hoots and whistles. He stomped to the footlights and in-cautiously bellowed, 'You hate me, don't you?' It was a question that would have been better unasked, for the re-sponse was a vociferous and morale-shattering, 'Well, we don't like you.'

To the sensitive Spike to whom the merest pin-prick was a stab to the heart, it was like a public execution. Distraught and humiliated he threw his trumpet to the floor and trampled it out of recognition. It was the only part of Milli-gan's act which drew genuine applause. He rushed off the stage with a wild look in his eyes and locked himself in his dressing room.

Sellers and Secombe who were dressed in Cockney garb festooned with bells for a sketch that was a send-up of a folk dancing competition, raced down the stairs and battered the door down. The prospect of suicide occurred to them because Milligan had been going through a macabre patch which in-cluded the purchase of a hangman's noose with a sick label saying 'only used once'. When the door finally gave way to their combined weights, they saw Milligan standing on a chair with the noose around his neck, and trying to hook it round an overhead pipe. Much later Sellers was to make the charitable observation that when Secombe screamed, 'For

God's sake, Don't do it, Spike,' Milligan gave them a slow wink.

Whether Milligan was joking or not, it certainly shook his partners. 'Poor old Spike was in a very bad way,' said Sellers. Certainly it was the beginning of the mental troubles that were to blight his life. Even today when his genius is recognized all over the world and there is no reason to doubt his own ability, something snaps and Milligan finds himself in the dark familiar tunnel of total despair. This is not the place to deal with his long history of breakdowns; it will be left to Spike's own section of the book in which he talks with brutal and revealing honesty about the tightrope he continually treads. Spike is his own best analyst.

The collapse at the Hippodrome was also a traumatic experience for Sellers who had never overcome his loathing for the music hall circuit. He hated to see the public humiliation of a man who was not only a creative genius but also a friend. In rage and contempt he deliberately set about cutting the hostile audiences down to size, by proving to them that *he* could dictate what *they* liked. In that bold decision Sellers revealed a tungsten-toughness that was lacking in Milligan. The next matinee after the Milligan debacle Peter scrapped his own act and substituted an unrehearsed parody of a 'visual disc jockey'. Clad in a misshapen leopard skin leotard he walked on stage carrying a record player and a 10-inch LP he had bought that morning of Wally Stott playing Christmas melodies. He bowed gracefully and said, 'Good afternoon. I'd like to play you some lovely melodies which I have enjoyed very much. I think you will like them too.'

Sellers put the needle on the record, pulling up a chair, cocked his head to one side and listened with a look of total entrancement on his face. He cut an incongruous figure in his crotch-sagging tights and the audience sat in bewildered silence as the music of Jingle-Bells and White Christmas flooded through the auditorium.

'At the end of the record, I clapped my hands, and they all joined in. I played three more records and left the stage to a terrific round of applause,' he recalled.

The wings were crowded with the rest of the cast who were completely mystified at the antics of the man who seemed intent on committing professional suicide. Had he, like Milligan, had a breakdown? Had the pressure of an hostile audience proved to be the last straw?

The theatre manager who found the rapturous applause akin to the sound of a cash register was not unduly alarmed, but the Hippodrome's owner was, and in no uncertain terms he told Sellers that he was to do his act 'as known', which in theatre jargon means he must perform the act for which he was booked. Sellers wasn't simply being bolshie, he was proving something; but he didn't argue. 'I couldn't repeat the act, but I had proved something to myself if to no one else. I'd proved that you can mould an audience to like anything – if you try hard enough.'

Secombe was among that nail-biting handful in the wings, but his concern soon turned to unstinted admiration. Sellers had taken on the audience at their own game and won hands down. His sheer professionalism and the courage to experiment made a lasting impression on the Welshman. 'Most performers would have gone out and knuckled down and accepted the brute supremacy of that audience. But Pete went out and gave them merry hell. It took a lot of guts.'

For a brief period Spike's career hung in the balance; he was told he would be reported to the London office. 'This will kill you in show business,' he was warned. Fortunately for millions of people, it proved an idle threat.

The tragic incident registered far more on Sellers than he cared to admit, and it was not long after this that he began to look towards the future which he saw in films and not as a Goon. 'I don't want to be a Goon all my life. They can't hang together much longer. It's got to end some time.' And he made the prediction that if he was to survive in any worthwhile sense it would be as a character actor.

When Milligan left the mental hospital after the Coventry drama and resumed normal life again he acted as if nothing untoward had happened. He plunged into more Goon Show scripts and continued to be the off-set prankster. One of his first calls was on Sellers, when dressed in a grubby raincoat and carrying a tray of matches he knocked on the door to inquire, 'Can I interest you in a thriving timber and sulphur business?'

The fact that Sellers opened the door wearing only a scarf and ammunition boots merely enhanced the view that Spike was back, bloody but unbowed.

The Goons were to stay together for six more years, during which time they scaled hitherto unknown heights of comedy. Their following grew and grew, and the public seemed to have an insatiable appetite as far as Goonery was concerned. Wisely, however, they decided to call a halt when they were at their peak. New vistas were opening for Sellers as a film actor, and Secombe was in great demand as a solo act. Milligan felt written out. 'The pressure and the tension of keeping up the standard drove me mad. I dedicated my whole life to it, seven days a week. Christ, it was terrifying! I used to get up, get to the BBC before nine, work right through the day and evening and get the last tube home. Sometimes I'd miss it and Peter would come and take me home in his car.'

And so The Goons made their final broadcast from the Camden Theatre on 28th January, 1960. It was appropriately titled, 'The Last Smoking Seagoon'.

John Browell, who produced the final shows, said, 'I was called in when the shows started to show signs of the old indiscipline edging back. We recovered the shape but the end was already in sight. The break-up was inevitable. Sellers was in demand both here and in America, and it was becoming increasingly difficult to get them together. I'm a great believer in stopping something before the public get tired of it, and although the public still wanted more it was a deliberate decision to end it.'

Like old soldiers The Goons refused to die or fade away. The public persisted in asking for more, but Milligan, Sellers and Secombe, their compasses set on the courses of individual stardom, resisted the clamour. But they couldn't, and never would, be able to shake off the title of ex-Goon no matter to what pinnacles they soared. For that matter they didn't want to. They continued to meet regularly to chat about old times and automatically lapse into that harlequinade of colourful characters they had created with such brilliance.

Secombe tried to explain it in a Backword to *The Goon Show Scripts*. He wrote, 'I wonder how many people realize how near we have become in real life to the characters we played. Scratch Peter and you find Bluebottle. Discard the trappings of the jet set and there he is – querulous in his Mum's old drawers, thinking lecherous thoughts about Gladys Twit and wearing boxing gloves to bed. Eccles lurks behind Spike's every move, liable to pop out at the most unlikely moments ... Spike thinks of me as Neddie. No matter what I do or to whatever theatrical or social aspirations I may pretend, he can see that beneath the finger-nail deep veneer of sophistication there lie the shattered underpants and tattered vest emblazoned with the Union Jack of Neddie Seagoon ...'

Or as he puts it less lyrically, 'We'd come alive on Sundays. It was like being let out of school.'

Sellers echoed his words. 'I can honestly say that it was the happiest professional period of my life. I never had such fun, enjoyment or fulfilment either before or since.'

Secombe, Sellers and Milligan are now stars in their own right, all burning with a brilliance that shows no sign of flickering or faltering. So why is it that although they have a limitless horizon ahead they continually keep peeping over their shoulders to those bye-gone days? It's not simply nostalgia.

To understand fully the magnetism The Goon Shows exercised on them we must take them individually and open them up like watches to see what makes them tick.

Chapter Four

MILLIGAN – TORTURED GENIUS

Some people (and the only Freud they've heard of is Clement) claim that you have only to look at Spike's childhood to get the key to his personality. It explains his inherent dislike of the Establishment, authority, injustice and oppression. It also accounts for his insistence that comedy is a social weapon and not simply laugh-raising escapism. There is more than a germ of truth in the claim, although it is not the complete answer. Like most things written and said about Milligan, it is an oversimplification. But it is beyond questioning that Spike's boyhood made him acutely conscious of colour prejudice, inherited privilege and bureaucracy, all of which have been constant targets for his satire. For he grew up in India in the dying days of the Raj, enjoying the luxury of servants and an outdoor life which most European youngsters had only read about in Rudyard Kipling. He swam in tropical rivers, kept a pet monkey, and lay at night listening to the growl of tigers in the jungle only a few yards away from his bedroom window. That part he loved. The regimentation and 'bull' of the military base where he lived, and the indifferent treatment of the natives, he detested. 'All that marching up and down and stamping of feet didn't seem to make much sense,' he said.

India, however, still exercises a deep fascination and some of his most memorable characters were drawn from his childhood memories. Those gouty old colonels in solar toupee are not figments of imagination; he encountered many of them in his childhood. Like Sellers, the past has a magnetic attraction for him and he once remarked fearfully, 'I'm an old Irish nostalgic. The past is so sweet and sad and beautiful for me.' But when one looks back at his peaks and troughs of life it is hard to understand what prompted the remark. The past was more sad than sweet.

The son of an Irish Sergeant-Major in the British Army, he was born Terence Alan Milligan in the Military Hospital at Ahmednaga on 16th April, 1918. Dad – Leo Milligan – was out on patrol most of the time and the young Milligan spent his formative years under the watchful eye of his mother Florence and an aunt. The thud of boots 'square bashing', and the raucous drill commands were never far off. He probably cut his teeth on a cartridge case, for both sides of the family had a long military history that stretched back to the Siege of Lucknow. The family picture album has an impressive portrait gallery of men in pill-box hats with waxed moustaches and jaws set in grim determination, and there are a few headstones in Indian military cemeteries bearing the family names.

If Milligan didn't share his father's liking for the martial he at least inherited his love of the theatre. Leo Milligan, a striking looking man, was known as 'India's Soldier Showman' and he frequently appeared alongside his wife at Military concerts. Spike made his debut at the tender age of seven when he played a clown in the school Christmas play; naturally it had to have its comic and controversial side. His face was painted blue, but for some inexplicable reason the small boy argued that it should be black. Neither could he understand why he was excluded from the final scene when the other tiny thespians in the cast crowded round the Virgin and Child. Precocious even then, he elbowed his way between the Three Wise Men and Joseph to become the first cap and bells jester to appear in a nativity play. That small incident gives some insight to his future attitude to life. He recalls with clarity his reaction: 'I saw that everybody else was there, and I thought the clown should have a place in life.'

Spike learned to speak Urdu and remembers this period of his life, and the Indian people, with a great deal of affection. 'People there are warm and open and kind,' he said. 'Not at all like Britain, where they are closed and unfriendly, sometimes even hostile, towards strangers.'

His affinity with the Indians prompted him to remark bitterly many years later, 'My father believed in mowing down any black man who gave him trouble. He was a good man, but he happened to have been criminally wrong.'

The young Milligan's love-hate world ended unexpectedly in 1933 when a ten per cent cut in the Armed Forces was ordered by the Government. Sergeant-Major Milligan was among those axed and at the age of forty, with no other profession than soldiering, he headed for England with his wife and two small sons, and a beggarly £2.10s. a week pen-

43

sion to keep them on. The blue skies of India were replaced by the grey skies and soot-grimed buildings of London. They moved into a Victorian terraced house at 4 Ringstead Road, Catford. There were no tigers but neither were there any rivers to bathe in.

The family's arrival in England, on a boat steaming up the Thames, provided a poignant and indelible memory for the impressionable fifteen-year-old Milligan, looking forward with awe and expectation to living in the land about which he had heard so much but never seen. But the arrival proved a disillusioning experience. 'I looked over the side of the ship, and there was a tugboat. I found a carnation and threw it into the tugboat, thinking a sailor might put it in his hat. He didn't. He crushed it with his heel. It was a lesson. England was much tougher, less sensitive; a land where you suppress your emotions.'

Apart from being a rather rash judgement, understandable in an extremely vulnerable teenager, it is in retrospect a typical Milliganism. Hurt by a crushed flower he condemned a whole nation out of hand. Nostalgia invariably tends to blur the edges of reality, but even in those days there seemed to be no subtle shades with Spike – just black and white, right or wrong. Ironically his acute sensitivity caused him to have blind spots. His detestation of the exploitation of native labour seemed to have blinkered him to the vicious treatment meted out to native by native in that caste-ridden land.

Overnight, life was transformed for the Milligan household. Instead of a servant-cosseted existence of comparative leisure, Mrs Milligan found herself literally slaving over a tiny stove trying to make ends meet with breakfast bubble-and-squeak made from yesterday's left-overs. 'It really broke me up,' he recalled. 'I retreated into a sort of dream world that I've been in ever since.'

One has to take that sweeping statement with more than a pinch of salt, but that times were hard there is no denying. Money was so scarce that Spike had to walk the three miles to St Saviour's Roman Catholic School in Lewisham twice a day, but so did many other kids, and it didn't scar them for life.

Leo Milligan may have been on his beam ends, but he refused to show it; he invested five guineas of his meagre savings on a made-to-measure pin-stripe, kid gloves and cane, and set out to find a job. Britain, unfortunately, was in the stranglehold of the Depression and bosses were not over impressed by the martial-looking caller with no qualifications. In desperation he took a job selling photographs for a Fleet Street news agency at a £2.10s a week salary that barely kept their heads above water. (He was later to improve his lot by taking a commission in the Ordnance Corps in World War Two and rising to the rank of Captain, although he had to borrow the money to buy his officer's uniform. Such things only served to increase Spike's dislike of the Army.)

Having come from a world where he had abhorred the 'sweated labour', the young Milligan ironically found himself employed as a 'wage slave' in a tobacco firm near Ludgate Hill where he worked from eight until six for thirteen shillings a week. He remembers it as 'a grey, grey world, putting cigarettes into packets, and the packets into bundles', and where every plea for an increase was met with a stubborn refusal. Times were hard for everyone, was the stereotyped answer.

The state of near-penury thwarted the burning ambition that occupied every waking moment. Beneath the cowed exterior of a fag-packer beat the heart of an aspiring Louis Armstrong. 'More than anything else in the world I wanted a trumpet.' With simple, if illegal, logic he reasoned out his next move. 'They're paying me a miserable wage, so I'll take a Robin Hood attitude and rob the rich to pay the poor. Meaning me.' It was Milligan's first and last foray into the twilight world of crime. He put aside some of the cigarettes he should have packed and sold them to his pals at knock down prices. From the proceeds, he put down a deposit on a glistening £25 trumpet and began paying off the instalments at thirteen shillings a week. He admits that he gave no thought to the legality of his under-the-counter transactions. 'It was just that the only way I could see to get that trumpet was to adjust the difference in wealth between that tobacco firm and young Terry Milligan,' he said. Unfortunately, his crime was unearthed when he was caught with some of the pilfered cigarettes in his pocket. The law had different ideas about what was permissible and what wasn't when it came to self-advancement, and the terrified youth was hauled before a juvenile court after spending two sleepless nights awaiting the hearing. The scene resembled the famous 'When Did You Last See Your Father' painting with a timorous Spike facing his inquisitors. The only difference was that Leo Milligan was present in the flesh to make an impassioned appeal on his son's behalf. 'He was only trying to improve his life,' he pleaded. 'We haven't any money, and he knew nobody else was going to give him some. He knew the firm wouldn't go bankrupt.'

There's no record of whether or not Spike revised his views of the heartless British after the magistrate let him go with a ticking off. We do know, however, that he lost his job but kept the trumpet.

His entry into the music world did not exactly set Satchmo quaking in his shoes. He joined Tommy Bretell's Ritz Revels and blew his head off for ten shillings a session at Saturday night gigs at St Cyprian's Hall, Brockley. The group wore white coats with black lapels and was according to Spike 'held together by hair oil'. In between he did uninspiring jobs as a laundry scrubber, and as an unskilled labourer at Woolwich Arsenal where presumably he would have stayed but for the intervention of Adolph Hitler and World War Two. A hernia and a slipped disc delayed his call-up, but in June 1940, Tommy Brettel lost his best trumpeter and the Arsenal its most uninterested worker. Gunner Milligan Number 954024, reported for duty to the 56th Heavy Regiment, Royal Artillery, at Bexhill-on-Sea, Sussex. As he strode through the gates, he carried his trumpet under his arm.

It was clear from the start that Spike was not going to take the war too seriously; anyway it was mouldering in that state which everyone dubbed 'the phoney war'.

The whole thing had seemed unreal to him, and he summed up his attitude in the first volume of his autobiography: 'A man called Chamberlain who did Prime Minister impressions spoke on the wireless; he said, "As from eleven o'clock, we are at war with Germany."' Spike accepted it without too much questioning, and later found himself stationed in an evacuated girls' school. The one time laundry scrubber was immediately made to feel at home; he was handed a brush and bucket of water and quick-marched into the cookhouse and told to put a shine on the floor that would have done credit to a guardsman's boots. Unfortunately, he had to do it wearing his 'civvies', a blue suit, the only one he owned. Crawling around on all fours not only put him in peril of 'housemaid's knee', it also wore out the knees of his precious trousers, and the uniformless Milligan cut a sorry and far from commanding figure when he did guard duty with his bony, white kneecaps exposed to the cold night air. Until the uniform shortage was overcome he was shifted to less conspicuous duties which did not detract from the dignity of His Majesty's Armed Forces.

While the British Expeditionary Force was being evacuated from Dunkirk a frustrated Milligan sat in a wooden observation post overlooking the Channel awaiting the threatened German invasion, all prepared to repel it with a rifle and five rounds of ammunition. The knowledge that he was expected to share those five rounds with everybody else in the post didn't instil in him a great deal of faith in the 'first line of coastal defence' of which he was such a vital part.

His confidence ebbed even more when he became a member of the gun's crew of a vintage World War One 9.2 howitzer which had everything except ammunition. A zealous officer overcame this trivial obstacle by getting the men to shout 'bang' as they did their gun drill. Milligan, ever the one to see the serious side of any comic situation, was reduced to helpless laughter at these morale-boosting exercises.

When it was announced that a carefully hoarded missile had been found that actually fitted the gun, there was jubilation among the hoarse-voiced gunners. Special permission was obtained from Southern Command HQ to fire into the sea and Milligan, realizing that such unaccustomed and violent activity might come as a shock to the residents of tranquil Bexhill, became a sandwich man. The day before the long-awaited shoot he and his pals paraded through the streets holding aloft posters which proclaimed: THE NOISE YOU WILL HEAR TOMORROW AT MIDDAY WILL BE THAT OF BEXHILL'S OWN CANNON. DO NOT BE AFRAID.

It was like a scene from Clochmerle as the citizens thronged the front for the historic occasion. The Artillery Officer resembled a pouter pigeon as he stepped forward for his proudest moment of the war. What followed could have been written by Milligan.

Seconds before the order to 'Fire', a lone rower stopped right in the middle of the target area to casually toss out a line and start fishing. A second rowboat was immediately launched to clear the offending fisherman. When the order to 'Fire' did finally echo across the still waters the shell turned out to be a dud. It was back to simulated explosions for the deflated gunners.

If nothing was happening in Bexhill things were certainly happening in the skies above, so Milligan volunteered for a transfer to the Brylcream boys in the RAF, but he was turned down and forced to accept the boredom and bulletless environment of Bexhill. He whiled away his time playing his trumpet and developing his mania for sticking irreverent notices on every available wall and door. (It's a fetish he still has.) The hand-written notices listed his fees for special recitals from his trusty trumpet, 'Fall in' was a shilling, 'Fall out' 1/6d, 'Retreat (Fortissimo)' 10/-, while the welcome notes of 'Halt' were on sale for £648.

It was all harmless idiotic fun, but Milligan's urge to express himself in comic turns was becoming more and more evident. Later when the 56th moved to North Africa, the most popular daily reading in the camp was his news bulletin called 'Milli-News' which he pinned up outside his tent. A typical communique said: 'Libya: Last night under cover of drunken singing, British Commandos with their teeth blacked

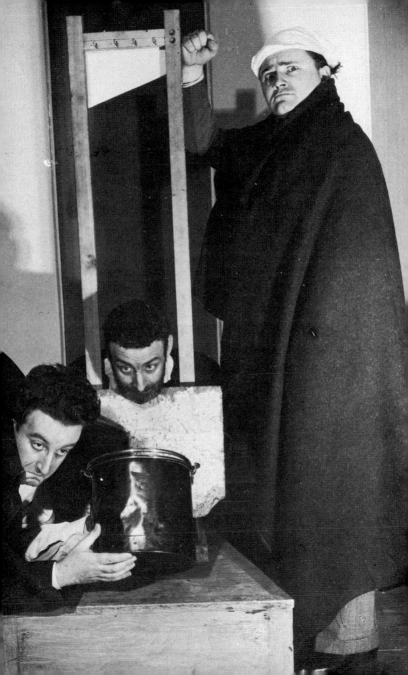

Above Sellers, Secombe, Milligan and Bentine record a 1951 Goon Show with bespectacled Mystery Guest. *Below* Ray Ellington, the gravel-voiced singer of countless broadcasts.

Above Lighting up with leeks for St David's Day, 1956. *Below* A serious mood — well, nearly — in 1958.

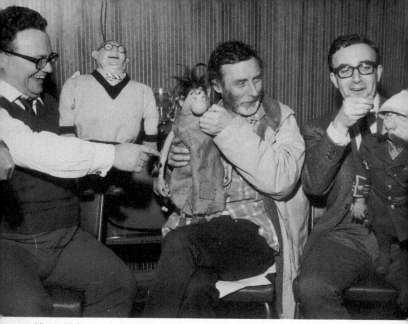

Above Telegoons (from left) Ned Seagoon, Eccles and Bloodnok. *Below* Christmas 1974, and the Goons go busking in London's Oxford Street. They raised £4.74 . . . and got moved on by the police.

In 1972 the trio re-assembled — for the first time in twelve years — to make a special Goon Show on the BBC's 50th birthday.

Above Royalty backstage after the anniversary show. Standing, from left: announcer Andrew Timothy, Lord Snowdon, Princess Margaret, Princess Anne and the Duke of Edinburgh. *Below* With Prince Charles at the Eccentrics Club.

Sellers and Princess Margaret leave Ronnie Scott's famous Soho jazz club.
Sellers quipped: 'We're just good friends.'

Michael Bentine: the Goon that got away.

out, raided an advance Italian laundry, several vital laundry lists were captured, and a complete set of Marshal Gandolfo's underwear, which showed he was on the run.'

Milligan's wit was worth a battalion of crack troops: when you can get men to laugh at the enemy the war is half won. They doubled up when they read: 'Rome: Il Duce told the Italian people not to worry about the outcome of the war. If they lost, he had relatives in Lyons Corner House, from whence he would run the Government in Exile.'

Milligan had a far from comfortable or 'soft' war. He saw a lot of action and was injured badly, but his memoirs* make it sound one glorious romp. The bullets and shells were real but Spike's recollection of it was not. He clouded the blood and sweat with a side-splitting humour that make his autobiography a must for anyone who wants to penetrate his protective kernel of buffoonery and get to grips with the real Milligan. From the deliberately distorted account a sharply defined portrait of Spike emerges.

His trumpet and way-out humour threw him together with Gunner Harry Edgington, a piano-playing jazz addict who also shared Spike's taste in literary slapstick. Unwittingly Edgington, a lanky sleepy-eyed Londoner, may have been responsible for planting the seeds of Goonery in Milligan's fertile imagination. Spike quotes this sample of Harry's writing in the first volume of his own as yet unfinished trilogy. 'The door flew open and in crashed the master-spy himself, Gruenthaphartz, measuring five rounds gun-fire by inches three, and clad only in a huge fur coat of huge fur, a sou'-wester, and two hand-painted barges strapped to his feet for a quick getaway. With a hairy on the knee. He was escorted by a plaque of Zeppelins. He loped across the room with a great lope and snatching up a sharpened lamp-post hurled it wildly at the bedraggled portrait of Sir Bennispon-of-du-Whacka. "So perish all my enemies" he roared . . .'

Milligan joined Edgington in churning out scores of similar

* *Adolph Hitler – My Part in His Downfall* and *Rommel? Gunner Who?* both published by Michael Joseph.

49

scripts for a non-existent audience, and they even began to write in sound effects.

In time Milligan was to hone and refine his talents until he produced the inimitable Goon scripts. Significantly it was around this time that Spike added the word Goon to his vocabulary. The *Daily Mirror*, which prided itself on being 'the Soldier's Paper', was running a Pop-eye cartoon series featuring some weird cerebrally-senseless and featureless characters who could do no right. From that moment Spike dubbed anyone he thought was an idiot as a 'Goon'. It was a craze which spread through the camp and 'in' members called themselves 'The Clubbers'. In moments of idle recreation they would whoop round the camp brandishing wooden clubs which they labelled 'Ye Crust Modifiers', lashing out at trees and bellowing 'Death to the Goons'. The riotous era ended when an officer found them sozzled, and naked, running through the Sussex woods shouting 'Viva Joe Stalin'. The clubs were destroyed in a hair raising ceremonial ritual when they were piled on to a railway truck, set on fire, and pushed down a sleeping line to their demise in a rubbish dump.

Despite his protestations to the contrary, Milligan was a good soldier, but then as now he was totally incapable of curbing his irrational sense of humour or holding his tongue. He would enlist his pals in laying 'saluting traps' for rank-conscious officers. At ten second intervals a man would walk past the officer and 'whip off' a smart salute. In a matter of minutes the arm-aching officer would be reduced to wondering where, in that man-starved army, they were all coming from.

Once on an exercise, when he was rebuked for not having his pike with him, he told a purple-faced officer, 'There didn't seem much point when I don't have any ammunition for it.' This earned him fourteen days in Preston Barracks, Brighton, and only added fuel to his smouldering contempt for senseless regimentation. He weeded the parade ground, assembled lumps of coal in neat and orderly piles, and saluted anything that moved and wasn't painted white.

It was in the army that he acquired the *nom de guerre* that was later to go up in lights in preference to his real Christian name. In between route marches, spud bashing and gun drill, he and Edgington earned a little extra cash to supplement their army pay by forming a band and playing at weekly dances in the Old Town Church Hall in Bexhill, and the Hailsham Corn Exchange. When they realized their music was inhibited by the absence of a double-bass they 'borrowed' one from the town's De La Warr Pavilion and smuggled it out in a crate stencilled 'Mark Three Bofor Gun Spares'. Clearly any lesson he had learned from the trumpet incident at the cigarette factory had long since been forgotten. Trumpeter Milligan was nicknamed 'Spike' by an ardent fan of Spike Hughes; although Milligan's musical ability did not measure up to the maestro's, it was as near as the fan could get to his idol. The name stuck.

Dixie Dean, a jazz drummer, now the service manager for a Hailsham television retail and rental company, later poached Spike for his own group; he turned back the pages of his memory to recall his musicianship. 'When I first saw him he was really getting into the music and unashamedly hogging the middle of the stage. With every note he forced from his trumpet, he leaned back in his chair, coming forward to bang his feet on the boards. I had a few rows with him over music because he hated playing popular stuff. His pet hates were the Warsaw Concerto and In the Mood, the Glenn Miller hit which was all the rage those days. We were forever being asked to play it and each request brought a look of horror and disgust to his face. I told him we were being paid to play popular music, and popular music was what we would play. But anyone who played music he didn't like was a Goon.'

Apart from an insight into Spike's taste in music, it reveals that even then he was intolerant of toeing the line and providing the conventional and safe.

Dean interpreted it a different way. 'This attitude was all part of his general rebelliousness and disdain for authority which came out in almost everything he said and did. He even managed to turn the wearing of his forage cap into an act of defiance. Most of the blokes wore them slightly to one side of their heads; his was worn dead centre and pulled down over his ears as far as it would go.'

Surprisingly Dean didn't see Milligan as an aspiring comic using his army mates as a captive audience for his shafts of wit. 'I don't think he intended to be funny or make people laugh. He just had satirical, outlandish thoughts which gave him a different view of life, and to us they came across as funny.'

Dean cited an example to prove his point. 'He had this outlandish scheme of us all getting together after the war and setting up a nightclub on a boat outside the three mile limit and away from any interference from the law. A grandiose scheme for a bloke who didn't seem to own anything except his trumpet. But that was Spike, happily bouncing through life in a world of crazy schemes and dreams.'

Dixie was surprised when the war ended that Spike didn't take up music as a career for he once auditioned for the BBC Rhythm Club and was picked as the best trumpeter. His reward was to cut a disc with George Shearing, the blind pianist. But fate was already conspiring to ensure that he became a comic. Nothing seemed to happen to him that hadn't been plotted by some omniscient script writer. During an exercise Milligan was instructed to send off the following signal: 'Invasion Fleet in the Channel, two miles off Seaford, steaming N.W. Estimated strength three capital ships, sixteen destroyers, and lesser craft.' By a quirk of fate, or perhaps a lousy system of communications, the signal went direct to Corps Headquarters instead of Regimental HQ. Panic stations ensued. The War Office visualizing the Invasion had started wanted to know if the Royal Navy had been alerted, for it looked as if Britain had been caught with her trousers down. An inquest was held and a shame-faced Milligan had to confess that he had omitted the ultimate but most vital word of his signal – 'Practice'. Not since the Good Soldier Schweik had an army had such an accident-prone hero.

Before Spike had a chance to make any more demoralizing

blunders he was shipped with 10,000 other troops to Algeria and there the war started in earnest. Soon after this came the encounter that many consider as historic as that other African meeting that began so formally with 'Doctor Livingstone I presume'. Milligan met Secombe. The manner of that meeting has already been recounted, but the two men impressed upon the minds of their superiors that the calamitous confrontation was not merely a 'one-off' incident. Soon afterwards the Irishman and Welshman were to stage an encore. It happened when Milligan, who was driving along a narrow mountain road in Italy, spotted Secombe ahead in another jeep. Harry did a sharp left-hander in response to a sign which read 'to the Bridge'. Spike, anxious for a few words, followed in hot pursuit. Unfortunately, unknown to them, the engineers had only erected one half of the pontoon bridge and had laid a smoke screen to disguise the fact from the enemy. Secombe went through the smoke in top gear and did a poor imitation of Evel Knievel by trying to leap the pontoonless gap. He and the jeep disappeared with an enormous splash. Milligan hearing the depth-charge explosion managed to stop inches from the edge, just in time to see Harry's dripping head pop up. 'He was livid,' recalls Milligan, 'and he asked a very rude question about the rest of the bridge.' The Keystone Cops would have been hard-pressed to improve on that.

But a far-from-comic occurrence was to take place soon afterwards and it was one which was to have a tormenting influence on Milligan for the rest of his life. The army was advancing on the seemingly invulnerable monastery at Monte Cassino and the enemy fire was murderous. Milligan took shelter in a small olive grove, and like all soldiers in moments of danger he rummaged for his cigarettes. Seconds later he was hit by a mortar shell. His own words capture the horror of that moment far better than anybody else's. 'I was counting out my Woodbines and reached five when this weird sound hit my ears. I can't describe it. It was like a razor blade being passed through my head. The next I remember, someone was giving me a cup of tea in a forward dressing station, but my hands were trembling so much I couldn't hold it.' Shrapnel had torn a massive hole in his leg and blasted his whole nervous system. He was so badly wounded and shell-shocked that he was pulled out of the front line and sent to base hospital. Later when he rejoined his regiment he realized that he was far from cured. Every time the guns opened up he developed a chronic stutter. As a wireless operator that made Milligan US. 'I'd had a considerable shock to my system and it made me a neurotic with a chronic anxiety state and the shakes. I still haven't got over it, and the Army pays me a partial disability pension,' he recalled later. 'When I get very uptight I stammer and have hardly any resistance to mental pressure. An unkind word can plunge me into the deepest gloom for a weekend and depress me so much that I cannot work at anything. I have to shut myself away from the world until I recover.'

After such an experience one can understand why Milligan chose to write his autobiography the way he did. The hilarious chronicles cocooned him from the stark realities of war. Only occasionally is the mask allowed to slip. 'I couldn't stand war and fighting. Violence was repugnant to me, and still is. I lost a lot of my mates, and it was nothing to laugh at really.'

By some quirk of fate Secombe was also wounded; if he hadn't been it is extremely unlikely that his and Milligan's paths would ever have crossed again. In that gory campaign thousands of men met fleetingly, but like ships that pass in the night never saw each other a second time. But Secombe fully recovered from his physical wounds was sent to a rehabilitation camp and there he met Spike who was healed bodily although still far from whole mentally. But at least they were spared the ordeal of any more action. The war in Europe had ended with the unconditional surrender of the Germans. Milligan and Secombe, who had spent so much of their off duty time making their pals laugh could now get down to the job with the full approval and blessing of the authorities. They joined the troops entertainment circuit. Milligan's recollection of it is a sophisticated parody of the hoary old army story of musical volunteers being needed – to shift a piano.

Recalls Spike, 'A crippled sergeant in a wheelchair came round and asked, "Does anyone do entertainments?" "I do," I said. "Make me laugh," ordered the sergeant. I told four jokes which produced no reaction whatsoever. So I picked up an axe and struck Harry Secombe. You should have heard the laughter then!'

They opened their partnership in the Officers' Club in Naples where Milligan, ever loth to toss away good material, repeated his mock axe attack. Harry sang 'Ah, Sweet Mystery of Life' to Spike's trumpet accompaniment. 'His performance had to be seen to be believed,' recalls Spike, and one waits for the deflationary punch line, but it doesn't come. 'He was the funniest man I had ever met. In fact, in those early days after my shell shock, I think he did more for me than all the doctors.'

For a year Milligan entertained forces audiences for the Combined Services Entertainment and even after his demob he still continued as a 'civvy' playing the trumpet with a jazz group, the Bill Hall Trio.

Harry Secombe said, 'A sort of alchemy had begun to work on the tour. We used comedy material culled from listening to soldiers talk, to which we added a special sort of whimsy. I doubt if we really succeeded in putting across our off-beat brand of humour, but almost without realizing it we were giving birth to the Goons.'

Hitler has been condemned, vilified and castigated more than any person in history, but at least he did one thing for which the world must be grateful – he saved Milligan from total obscurity. 'If it were not for him, I would probably have gone on to become a foreman at Woolwich Arsenal – and wondered why I was unhappy. When the war ended, I was a changed man. I was making a living with a highly-rated jazz trio and planning a future in show business.'

The gravy-wagon was still a long, long way out of reach, though. For a brief spell after the war, Spike and Harry and Norman Vaughan, a budding comic with a lugubrious expression, together with musician Johnny Mulgrew, another Service pal, shared a pad in Notting Hill. As there was only room for two and the landlord didn't approve of overcrowding, they were forced to resort to a little subterfuge before finally settling down for the night. As two went upstairs to the tiny room the others remained at the foot of the steps bellowing an unnecessarily loud 'Good night' before slamming the front door. Seconds later one would tip-toe down and readmit them. It was cheating, but when money was so scarce there was no alternative. Once Harry and Spike had to do a moonlight flit through the back window of some lodgings because they didn't have the rent.

In England the trio Spike was with began a variety tour which took in most of the theatres in the North, but the winter of 1948 was marked by heavy snow, bitter cold and an acute fuel shortage. The endless trudge from town to town, digs to digs, made life a grim and miserable affair. Theatres were often half empty and so the group headed south for the bright lights of the West End where they did the rounds of the nightclubs. It was a hectic life of double dates which meant scrambled dashes from one venue to another without even time to remove their make-up. Spike threw it in and went to work at The Grafton Arms as a barman, not realizing that he was taking the first step towards showbiz immortality.

As a barman Spike was a superb joke-teller, and Jimmy Grafton soon had him making the odd contribution for the scripts he was himself writing for Derek Roy and other comedians. It was then that The Grafton Arms began to become a morale-boosting haven for ambitious but as yet unrecognized entertainers. Milligan, the two-fingered touch typist, found himself writing material for the up and coming comedian Alfred Marks, and getting the odd bit of extra cash for sitting in the audience as his stooge. Marks, now an international star, said, 'I kept some of Spike's old scripts for years, and always laughed like a drain when I read through them. But at that time, I thought his material was too far out for the audiences.'

When Sellers, Secombe and Bentine burst upon the scene they had no such qualms and as has already been told, the four worked with dogged perseverance and tenacity to batter down the barricades of hide-bound conservatism which prevented them getting on BBC radio. The epoch-making breakthrough came after that first broadcast, and although it caused no more than a ripple of interest it had decided Milligan where his future lay. 'At thirty-three, I had discovered what I really wanted to do in life – write comedy.'

Even if those early shows didn't bring overnight success or instant wealth, they provided Spike with an all too short period of physical and intellectual content. 'They were the most original comedy shows the world has seen,' he said with an uncharacteristic lack of modesty. 'They represented a great release in those post-war years for people who didn't want formality and routine. We did the mad ideas that Peter and I used to sit up half the night discussing. We did our own sound effects. For example: "Knock! Knock!" – "Who's there?" – "A short man who can't reach the knocker." We also did an unheard of thing on radio. We presented a man who sold silences. "Would you like a silence this long————? Or this long————? Or this long————?" They asked for sound effects the BBC had never been asked for before. Such as a Wurlitzer organ being trundled across the Sahara desert, the pace of the music swelling with the engine revs. Playing a wave-tossed piano across the Channel. A wall being driven away at high speed.

Spike was in his element; a whole new world of comedy to explore, and a reasonably free hand with which to exploit it, although there were always one or two doubting Thomases murmuring in the background, 'He's gone too far, he must be curbed.'

The Goons did not make Milligan a rich man. For that first show he got £12 for his contribution to the writing, plus £8 performance money. A considerable time elapsed before he began to get 100 guineas for a script and £75 as a performer. But money wasn't a matter that occupied much of his attention. He was perfectly content to slog through an eighteen hour day on a 2/9d lunch in a carman's pull-up. Milligan's proud father went around telling everyone how well his son was doing, although in actual fact he was earning more money. It was only when Spike heard that Secombe and Sellers were getting more money that he asked for, and got, an increase. Significantly that was prompted more by personal pride than anything else. 'I think money is a hangup. I've never wanted it. It's just that you, well, need it,' he said many years later when money had become the least of his problems.

The scripts poured out of him like a cascade of precious gems. 'The Dread Batter Pudding Hurler', 'The Kippered Herring Gang', 'The Phantom Headshaver of Bexhill', 'The Hunt for the Wild Christmas Pudding' that held everyone at bay with its vicious antlered holly. It was difficult for anyone to imagine that such a labour of love was exacting a nerve-destroying toll, although Eric Sykes who co-operated on some of the early scripts remarked, 'He did on his own a job which would normally be handled by six or seven men.' But that was a comment made in awe rather than the remark of a man who sees the writing on the wall long before anyone else.

Coventry and its Hippodrome were, alas, just around the corner. The slight cracks in Spike's fragile armour were to widen into terrifying chasms.

Dixie Dean his old musician pal from army days recalls meeting him at the Winter Gardens, Eastbourne, and how surprised he was to hear Spike say, 'I don't believe the audience comes to see me. They don't like me. It's Harry they come to see.' It wasn't envy on Spike's part, it was a tragic lack of self-confidence. Dixie also remembers an after-the-show get-together at which Spike became nostalgia personified. He resurrected the improbable scheme for a floating casino moored outside territorial waters. 'He turned to me,' said Dixie, 'and asked, "Where did we go wrong? What happened to us and our plans?" I saw him on a number of occasions during this period, and he always had that haunted, weary look and a tension about him which was in stark contrast to the relaxed and sparkling man I had known before. He said he found it harder and harder to keep up the flow of new ideas.'

Yet despite the mounting pressures, Spike masochistically accepted a flood of commissions from other top comics for whom he now represented the 'in' writer. They hoped a little of his magic would rub off into their acts, much the same as some stars had been only too grateful for the laughter that was edited out of The Goon Show.

Spike was by now married to June Marlowe, an attractive young girl introduced to him by the actress Anne Howe who was to become the first Mrs Sellers. The four of them had partnered each other at a Water Rats' Ball at the Dorchester Hotel.

Milligan's crack-up, when it did come, was far worse than anyone who had seen the strain Spike was under could possibly have envisaged. Forgivably, many of them believed that Spike's white-heat industry was an integral part of his genius, completely manageable and under disciplined control, similar to the icily controlled frenzy of a jazz drummer. At one time such a breakdown was only talked about in hushed whispers, as to the general mind there was something obscene about them. Thankfully we are now more enlightened and compassionate, and Milligan has used his own personal problems to great therapeutic effect on others who have similarly suffered. He has written and talked about his own illness with such startling candour that one feels his survival owes a lot to his ability to dissect himself with such ruthless honesty.

Reading his own account of the personal disaster is like watching a slow burning fuse inching towards a powder keg, yet Spike seemed incapable of snuffing it out by simply taking a rest. He was wrestling with the Goon scripts and battling with people at the BBC who did not understand what The Goons were trying to achieve. His parents had emigrated to Australia and he feared he would never see them again. Instead of sleeping he was writing for comics he didn't have the heart to refuse. In addition, his wife was pregnant and he was flat hunting in London at a time when the chances of finding unfurnished accommodation was as likely as striking oil in Hyde Park. But when he did find a home the pressures increased instead of decreasing.

After the baby, Laura, was born his wife developed post-natal fever and he was stuck in a three-bedroomed flat with a two-week-old-baby. He had to get a nurse, then a bed for her. And all the time work was piling up. 'It was a nightmare. My crack-up came from overwork, professional problems, and responsibility thrust on to a personality unprepared to bear it. The madness built up gradually. I found I was disliking more and more people. Then I got to hating them. Even my wife and baby. And there were the noises. Ordinary noises were magnified in my brain until they sounded a hundred times as loud as they were, screaming and roaring in my head. Footsteps were like hammer blows, the scratch of a match became the sound of rending metal in a train crash. I began to suspect everyone was my enemy, criticizing me, maligning me, closing in for the kill. I could feel my eyes flashing from side to side like those of a haunted animal. And the process is so insidious that the awful thing was that I had no idea I was mentally sick.'

Spike was writing after the event. At the time he thought he was the only one in step; it was other people who were odd. Surprisingly he was going through a creative bonanza, he was writing faster and funnier than at any time in his life. It resembled the sudden extra brilliance a light bulb gives out before the filament goes. At times his head felt as if it were under a welder's torch, and apart from the persecution complex he began to think that no one, not even those closest and dearest to him, appreciated what he was going through. As for the doctors, all they did was give him sleeping pills. Although he continued to write he neglected himself; he stopped shaving and let his hair grow down to his shoulders. Never a fastidious dresser at the best of times, his appearance became so bad that when a man from the agency which had rented the flat called, he almost fainted when Milligan opened the door.

Milligan was like a pressure cooker with a stuck valve. 'I thought: "Nobody is on my side. They are letting me go insane. I must do something desperate so they will put me in hospital and cure me. I know what I'll do. I'll kill Peter Sellers."'

Why he should have picked on Sellers he has never explained. Probably it was because he was the most conveniently placed; he was living in a next-door flat in Highgate. When Sellers called round to borrow a record player Milligan decided the ideal moment had arrived. He picked up a potato knife, put it in his dressing-gown pocket and went into the living room and tried to kill Sellers. 'What exactly happened I can't clearly remember, but I do remember shouting: "I'm going to kill Peter Sellers." If I had meant it, I would have said, "I am going to kill you, Peter." I recall the ambulance taking me to St Luke's Hospital in Highgate.'

The 'murder attempt' had at least paid off. That it was no more than a desperate move to draw attention to his illness is beyond question – no one in their right mind would choose a potato knife for the lethal instrument.

At the hospital the doctors were surprised that he hadn't been admitted earlier and it was just as well that Milligan was in no fit state to tell them of his attempts to get into hospital. Rest was what he clearly needed and he was treated with sodium amytal, but it didn't work; Milligan stayed awake brooding over imagined grievances and working out plots to get revenge on his non-existent enemies.

'In the end, I imagined even my wife was against me. I would shrink from her, screaming in terror, refusing to let her touch me. I was truly a raving lunatic.'

Finally they did manage to put him into a drugged sleep, but when he woke up he began to have hallucinations. The ceiling became a swirling kaleidoscope of violent colours, a roaring lion would appear and leap on to his bed and start clawing his chest and face. The harbinger of evil, the raven, would fly through the closed window and write Biblical texts

61

in Hebrew on the wall with its beak. Tennyson's Lady of Shallot, with long gold tresses to her waist and wearing a white flowing robe, would materialize at the foot of his bed and talk to him. The Crucifixion was enacted before his eyes and he would scream in horror, 'You are killing the wrong man' and Christ's blood would spurt all over him. He would jump out of bed and pound on the door shouting 'I am clean.'

Suddenly there came a turning point and a calmer, no longer hysterical Milligan asked for a Bible which he read for hours on end until a sense of peace took over. When he gazed in the mirror he looked like Ben Gunn, his hair and beard were grey and unkempt, and he thought he had been in hospital for years. When he demanded some newspapers his suspicions deepened. Had they given him comparatively old ones to disguise the length of his illness? In fact he had been in hospital a matter of weeks, not years. But he was far from cured and when his wife came along with the baby and the family pet he would only talk to the dog. 'It must have broken her heart. But she was a brick through it all, patient, smiling, affectionate.'

Gradually he began to write again, not long energy-sapping pieces but just the odd funny thought that occurred to him. 'Every night my little boy crawls across the floor to greet me when I come home from work. I'm very worried about him. Why? He's forty-two,' was a typical example.

When he discharged himself from hospital he went to live on a houseboat on the Thames, and there among the peaceful surroundings of the riverside and country he found tranquillity. Relaxed, his confidence restored, he once more felt capable of facing up to the rigours of life. When he returned home he was broke and Secombe, who had been helping Mrs Milligan to keep the home going, wrote out a cheque for the unpaid hospital bill which Milligan insisted on paying back despite Harry's protestations. 'I shall never forget that he was in the background all the time,' said Spike. Secombe's gesture revealed how deep and abiding was their friendship.

Milligan knew he was not completely healed, and for that

matter never would be. Whenever the pressure builds up he knows he is liable to another breakdown and so he has built protective barriers as a defence against them. He says he is a tougher person than he used to be. 'It was, and is, self-preservation. I decided I must never let people walk on me again because, if I did, I'd go out of my mind again.' (Out of his hearing friends say they haven't noticed any toughening; he's still far too generous and accommodating.)

Milligan's soul-baring is an obvious example. It took him a long long time before he could bring himself to talk about his illness, and when he did write about it he was thinking of others – not himself. 'I think,' he explained, 'people ought to know what it is like to have a nervous breakdown. Knowing what it is like, perhaps they will show more sympathy and understanding. There is nothing obvious about it, no blood, no bandages. People won't believe there is anything wrong with you. "Come on now, pull yourself together," they say, as if it's your own fault.' By chronicling his illness in such detail he hopes people who are heading for a breakdown will recognize the early symptoms and seek help.

Much later he went through the lacerating ordeal of re-living it all for a Granada TV documentary 'The Other Spike' which was made in an empty ward of a hospital. 'It was a chastening experience but I wanted people to know what it was like. So many people reach that stage, and usually no one around them understands.'

Milligan returned to The Goon Shows and his genius blossomed even more. It is difficult to understand why he returned considering what it had done to his health and sanity, and he only managed to survive by keeping a careful watch for the danger signals. Then he would ease up and take a rest cure. It was only in this way that he managed to keep writing so long and so brilliantly. When The Goons did finally end he lapsed into a state of lethargy that lasted nearly two years.

But before the curtain finally came down he took a trip to Australia to visit his parents. He had lost four stone in weight and his clothes were so ill-fitting he looked as if he had raided a scarecrow's wardrobe.

(It was through a piece of hidebound Foreign Office bureaucracy that Spike officially became Irish. During the visit to Australia he was curtly told that he didn't have any nationality. He wasn't British because he was born in India, and his father was born in Ireland. He could, however, apply for British nationality. Spike took umbrage and remained Irish.)

The family reunion worked wonders and his father managed to instil in him some of his own confidence in his ability: there was, he said, only one way Spike could travel and that was upwards. Spike was in fine fettle when the moment arrived for the homeward journey. He remained buoyant and in splendid spirits until the ship docked at Callao, in Peru, on the halfway stage of the voyage. Then the bottom dropped out of his world. A letter from his solicitor was waiting for him which contained the shattering news that his wife had left home with their three children and was suing for divorce. Milligan was hurt, but with typical candour admitted that he wasn't really surprised. Their seven-year-old marriage had been coming apart at the seams for some time, and his mental condition had aggravated the situation. He knew he had undergone a personality change which had made him nigh impossible to live with, and while he could accept his wife's decision the thought of losing his children proved too much to bear. He decided to end it all and commit suicide. He had a hot bath, put on clean pyjamas – 'a last attempt I suppose, at achieving the dignity of cleanliness' – switched off the light and swallowed a handful of sleeping tablets. There Milligan would have at last found the peace of mind which had so persistently eluded him – but for one thing: he had overlooked the fact that he had invited the ship's doctor to his cabin for a nightcap. A stomach pump was sent for and his life was saved. Whether or not he really had forgotten the doctor is a matter for conjecture. Either way, millions of people are grateful that the doctor liked a tipple.

When the ship docked at Southampton, Eric Sykes, the gangling comedian-writer who had co-operated in a number of early day scripts, was waiting on the quay to take him home. But the empty house was too full of memories and Milligan moved into his office and slept on the floor. The wheel had turned full circle since those Grafton Arms days.

Divorce courts are cold impersonal places where human tragedies are made so much worse by the remote matter-of-fact attitude of lawyers who are prepared to drag out everything in order to substantiate the grounds for a parting. For the still-far-from-well Milligan, it served to open up all the old wounds. The judge was told how, when he was in bed with one of his bouts of depression, he sent a telegram to his wife, who was in the same house, asking for a bowl of soup. One must sympathize with her for such impossible behaviour, but if Milligan had not been so mentally disturbed he would never have dreamed of doing it. The only consolation was that he was granted custody of the children.

A long period of 'resting' – that theatrical euphemism for being out of work – followed and salvation eventually came in the form of Sir Bernard Miles, the cider-voiced actor who runs the Thames-side Mermaid Theatre at Blackfriars. He offered Spike the part of Ben Gunn, the crazy cheese-eating castaway in 'Treasure Island'. Much as he wanted and needed work, Milligan was uncertain; he havered and insisted he was not an actor. Miles convinced him he was. That was all the assurance Milligan really needed, although he soon realized there were limits to his stagecraft. He found he could not dance and sing at the same time, so he compromised by dancing a few steps, then stopping and speaking a few lines of dialogue. The show not only became a money-spinner and award winner, but a perennial Christmas panto. More important, Spike emerged as a solo artist in his own right; he was not dependent on others for a livelihood.

That wasn't the only milestone. He met and fell in love with actress Patricia Ridgway. They were married at a Roman Catholic ceremony in a small church in a picture postcard Yorkshire village. Hundreds of people travelled to The Dales for the wedding in 1962 – among them Peter Sellers and Harry Secombe.

Milligan then proved that his success in 'Treasure Island'

65

was no flash in the pan; with John Antrobus he wrote 'The Bed Sitting Room', an almost Goon-like fantasy with a serious message. Due to its brilliant writing and Milligan's superb solo performance, it steered clear of being labelled propaganda, that rock of self-indulgence on which so many shows have floundered. It was Milligan at his irrepressible best. Wearing a Wee Willy Winkie nightgown and a drooping nightcap complete with bobble, he held the audiences entranced through three acts.

It was set in the aftermath of World War Three, which had lasted two minutes and twenty-eight seconds, including the peace treaty. The world had become a bed-sitting room at 29 Scum Terrace, Paddington, and Harold Macmillan, who was still Prime Minister, was turned into a parrot which was cooked and eaten in the last scene. God made a cameo appearance, dressed in his underwear, to be greeted with a cry of 'Good old Gawd! He's a Socialist, you know!' and a chorus of 'For he's a jolly good fellow'. God then announced that because of radiation in the celestial altitudes, the Kingdom of Heaven was to be re-established at 29 Scum Terrace, but blacks were to be barred. It was typically irreverent Milligan, proclaiming his dislike of race prejudice and fear of nuclear pollution under a blanket of humour. The Goonery stunts remained. When the play moved to the Duke of York's Theatre, he announced that the H-bomb in the play had been lost somewhere between the Mermaid and St Martin's Lane. 'If anyone finds a brown paper parcel, please open it,' he said. 'If London disappears, you've found it.' Even the unplanned calamities produced gales of laughter; for the audience, Milligan's inventiveness was limitless. One evening, at the end of the first act, he grabbed the curtain, was hauled twenty feet from the stage, and was stuck there because it had jammed. He hung on, hoping his weight would bring down the curtain. When it didn't, he pulled faces at the audience and whistled. They laughed and applauded, thinking his antics were all part of the show, while backstage there was panic to get the curtain down. After five minutes of fooling, Spike solved the problem by letting go and falling to the stage with a loud crash. He was unhurt, but he gave up grabbing the curtain.

Out of work again, Spike went into 'Son of Oblomov', a straight play which seemed destined for a brief run at the Lyric, Hammersmith. He forgot his lines on opening night, so ad-libbed everything. He recalls: 'I was insulting to everybody who appeared on stage. You'd get this pompous actor walking on and saying: "My dear Oblomov," and I'd answer: "Who sent this nit here?" I thought the drama wasn't much good, but it was funny.' 'Oblomov' got a panning from the critics, but Spike, who had asked his wife not to come to save his first night nerves, went home and told her it had been a success. He sweated over learning his lines properly, only to arrive at the theatre and find the other parts had been changed. So he made up his own lines, and his genius for improvization led to 'Oblomov' becoming the biggest success of the season and breaking records at the Comedy Theatre.

'When it became a success, I couldn't believe it,' he said. 'I'd made up my own part as a last desperate gamble. After all, I'd been booed off stage before, had things thrown at me in Scotland, and been stranded without money. So what was there to lose?' Some of the dialogue seemed to provide an excellent opportunity for ridicule. The leading lady said: 'What would you do if I died?' and Milligan replied: 'Bury you.' The line got a howl of laughter – but it must have been a terrifying experience for the legitimate actors to find the parts they were creating with dedication being shattered by his off-the-cuff remarks. When another character exclaimed: 'You know, girls always make me think of marriage,' Milligan retorted, 'Well, as long as boys don't, you're safe.'

He had not expected the play to run for more than a month and was astonished when his dresser, Tom Calder, who looked after Sid Field, took him aside to say: 'You're going to make it, son. I have never heard such laughter in the theatre since Sid was at his peak.' In spite of the success, money wasn't lavished on the production and Milligan decided to rectify the shortage. One night, when the leading lady

67

came on with holes in the sleeves of her dress, he marched to the front of the stage to ask, in front of a packed house, if she could have a new dress the next day. She got it. When he ripped open a pair of trousers in mid-show, he queried, 'Can I have a new pair tomorrow night?' and got them. He kept up the campaign. 'Can I have some buttons sewn on my waistcoat? ... The leading lady's wig is matted and dirty ... They can't hear at the back – can we have a microphone?' All asked from the footlights. And every request granted.

Prima donnish? Not in Milligan's eyes. 'I have no star complex. I always asked to have my name the same size as the rest of the cast. I'm not saying, "I'm ever so humble, sir." It's just that I like it like that. It seems to me the right relationship to have with my fellow men. I think I am very privileged to have been chosen to create laughter. I also think everybody in the theatre should fawn on the audience. They are the people who pay your rent and the school fees and all the rest.'

He did walk off stage once during 'Oblomov' as a measure of respect for the audience. The show was being wrecked by a party of hecklers who commandeered all the boxes. Spike decided to do something about it for he felt the audience was not getting value for money and were being taken for a ride because of the rowdies. He advanced to the apron and issued an ultimatum: 'Ladies and gentlemen, if these people can do better than I can, let them do it. I'm going home – and if I were you, I'd ask for my money back.' And, with that, he stormed off.

During one performance the Royal Family, all ardent Goon fans, took an active part in the ad-libbing with Sellers who was present as their guest. Milligan the arch anti-Establishment man was invited back to dinner leaving himself open to the criticism that he was prone to run with the hare and hunt with the hounds. But the relationship between The Goons and the Royal Family, so vastly different to the respectful badinage of those other court favourites, The Crazy Gang, is so unique that it deserves a chapter of its own.

Spike took a three-week rest from 'Son of Oblomov' in order to take his children on holiday, and the show had to close down till his return because there was no way of replacing the ad-libber. After all, even he didn't know his lines. When the show returned, an unappreciative American lady fell asleep and Milligan had the lights turned up while he sang the National Anthem to her. The audience loved it, but she didn't.

'Oblomov' occupies a treasured spot in his heart, the wolf had been driven from the doorstep with no possible hope of a return visit. In the first year he earned £40,000, the first *real* money he had ever made. His ego also enjoyed a tremendous fillip; the nightly applause drove away the uncertainties and he at last accepted that he was a clown *par excellence*.

When Milligan finally quit the show, he appropriately made the announcement from his bed on stage. He said, 'I've had enough of "Oblomov". I'm getting double vision. At weekends, the kids keep asking: "Who is that funny man?" ' Without him, the show's long run had to end, leaving behind the memory of an ordinary play turned into an off-the-cuff gem of surrealist drama by his eccentric, unpredictable genius. The glibly humorous farewell hid the fact that Milligan had begun to hear the warning bells which now regulated his life. The moment had come to bow out graciously.

For a change of pace, Milligan switched to television, appearing with Sir Michael Redgrave in a comedy series 'World of Beachcomber', based on the *Daily Express* satirical column by J. B. Morton. It was a return to Goon-type roles, playing characters like Dr Strabismus and the leader of the Filthistan Trio.

Later he teamed up again with Eric Sykes in the London Weekend Television comedy series 'Curry and Chips' written by Johnny Speight, creator of the arch-bigot Alf Garnett. Milligan's character, a Pakistani fly-boy immigrant, was almost a black Alf Garnett, painfully race and colour conscious, insisting that his name was Kevin O'Grady and that he came from Ireland. Sykes was an ideal foil as the white foreman. Milligan once again proved that the perfect weapon for exposing and demolishing prejudice was a good belly laugh. But he was never able to shed his schoolboy impishness and during one of his visits to Australia he really blotted his copybook. It is revealing if not particularly amusing.

Milligan had been a guest on a morning chat show, the 'Peter Young Morning Show', at the Australian Broadcasting Commission studios in Sydney, which finished seconds before the 11 a.m. news bulletin, and he stayed behind when newsreader Rod McNeil came in to read the news. McNeil solemnly started his three-minute bulletin: 'The Prime Minister, Mr McMahon, returned to Australia today...' Spike interjected, 'With Spike Milligan.' The startled McNeil went on to deal with a report on the safety record of Australia's international airline Qantas. Spike stepped in again, to say in his 'Eccles' voice, 'We have only had thirty crashes this year...' McNeil's next item was about a speech in the South Australian parliament, and Spike interjected, 'Where nobody was listening.' McNeil, struggling to suppress a fit of chuckles, brought the bulletin to a premature close. 'And that's the end of the news in brief,' he said. 'The next news will be broadcast at...' But before he could get off the air, Spike leaned forward to tell the listeners, 'They'll never make it, folks.' It is a broadcast the people of Sydney have not forgotten. But the head of the Commission was not so amused and called for an enquiry. Fortunately, by that time, Spike had slipped back to England where he broadcast a fifteen-minute programme on BBC 3 radio, warning of the dangers of red-haired people catching Dutch Elm disease. Official disapproval was avoided because the programme went out on April 1st, a day when even the BBC has a sense of humour.

His output as a writer and actor was prodigious and his versatility grew and grew. He even played Raquel Welch's husband in 'The Three Musketeers'. When he appeared in a scene in bed with her, he couldn't resist sending boastful telegrams to Harry Secombe and Peter Sellers. Books flowed from him like a breached dam: poetry, novels, a miscellany called 'A Dustbin of Milligan', and two volumes of his war reminiscences, which have had big sales and received laudatory reviews even from august journals like the *Times Literary Supplement*. As a contract writer for the Marty Feldman television shows, he has written mounds of material which have helped boost Feldman as an international comic. However, he prefers writing material which he can present in his own inimitable fashion. His recent television series, Q6, allowed him to give full vent to his crazy comic genius. And he combined his loathing of racism with comedy for the BBC TV series, 'The Melting Pot', which he wrote with Neil Shand, and features two illegal immigrants who come to London and can't find any white people, but do meet a Chinese man with a Cockney accent and a negro with a broad Yorkshire accent.

Sadly he can't implement his well intentioned resolutions to curb his work urge, but he has at least found a relaxing balm; he locks himself in his office and reads books on philosophy. 'My life is a lot better now,' he said in an interview at his Bayswater office, where he was sprawled in his chair, wearing a faded jeans-suit and flip-flops. 'Though I still get these mental blow-outs. I just go off my nut. It's terrifying because nobody can help me. Not my wife. Nobody. It's difficult to explain. And because it is mental troubles, there's no broken leg or anything like that I can show. Consequently, I get accused of being a temperamental Irish nit. I have psychiatric treatment all the time, but I'm stuck with these depressions. I've got to live with them. When they end, I can get up off the floor, but it takes a bit longer each time. But there is a good result from these periods of depression. They help me, as a clown, to reach people and make them laugh. I think it's because of the pain I suffer gives me more understanding of human beings. Writing still puts me under a lot of pressure, but performing is something different. That's like a holiday for me. I love it, especially when I'm on-stage and can sit there and make up my own lines as I go along. Performing is so therapeutic for me, as long as I don't

71

have one of my depressions on. I can give myself and enjoy seeing everybody have some fun.'

Sometimes the strain on Milligan is only just below the surface. In another interview in his cluttered, but somehow neat, office, he philosophized, 'I would not detest the human race if I didn't love them so much.' But his utterances are not always so rational or considered. He pointed at the burning electric light bulb and said, 'Somewhere some idiot in a bowler hat is totting up the amps. It's costing us money to bloody well sit here and breathe.' Then he picked up the telephone to tell his housekeeper, 'I want you to measure the children. I never know what size to order when I buy their clothes. Measure their arms, feet, chest, legs, everything.' He put the phone down but was back on it minutes later to tell the housekeeper, 'I've just realized that the kids may be playing with the electric clock in the airing cupboard on the landing. See that they don't.' Shortly after, he was on to her again. 'Take the baby to the clinic,' he ordered. 'She is underweight. I want a diet. Put it all down on paper.' And again, 'You must take the children to the zoo much earlier. They don't have enough time there. One pound for an hour is too expensive.'

His office is crammed with box files in which he has collected odd thoughts which he hopes might be useful some day. He calls them his 'mind furniture'. One file is labelled 'God. Ha! Ha!' He explained: 'I thought of writing a comedy version of the Bible. It must have been a very happy occasion when the world was created. I wanted to do the film with Peter Sellers, and make it a comic presentation of the Bible so it doesn't all belong to the moaning Jeremiahs. It would begin with the screen blacked out and this voice coming over, all Charlton Hestonish: "And in the beginning, there was Darkness..." Suddenly, a 40-watt bulb is switched on and there's Eccles rising out of his camp bed saying: "Who put the bloody light on?" The Sermon on the Mount would be done seriously, but I see Peter doing the miracle of the loaves and fishes as Jesus doing an imitation of Tommy Cooper. Everything going wrong. And the bit with the wine. I can just see Tommy Cooper doing that.

'I think it sounds a bit of endearing nonsense, and that's what British comedy is. Pure nonsense. I've got this hang-up that British comedy should be spontaneous. It is way ahead of everything else. There has been a great renaissance in our humour. That's what the Goon Show was. A renaissance.'

All the time one is acutely aware that no matter what he says it is always linked to his deep and anguished concern for his fellow beings and the world they inhabit. He watches with a feeling of gloom as he sees the world as we know it being destroyed around us. He doesn't, however, sit back impassive and cynical with an 'I told you so' look on his face. He has launched himself wholeheartedly into campaigns to preserve things as diverse as Victorian post offices and disappearing tribes in Africa. He is a prolific writer of newspaper letters all aimed at getting something done about his many causes. He is a member of all the anti-cruelty and anti-vivisection societies there are. Once he opted out of working professionally for two months to work for charities and other deserving causes. Instead of turning out gags and sketches, he prepared a lecture which he gave up and down the country on the preservation of Victorian buildings. He lamented, 'Our towns are being knocked down and turned into one vast Surbiton.' He cajoled artists and managers to make an LP record 'No One's Going to Change the World'. Harry Secombe, Bruce Forsyth, the Beatles, and others pitched in under his urging and the record made £15,000 for the World Wildlife Fund. He joined movements to save Tower Bridge, the Victorian gas lamps on Constitution Hill, and the now demolished Coal Exchange, which went to make way for a Thamesside traffic improvement. He said, 'It's so sad. It was a Victorian masterpiece, built in the days of true craftsmanship. It shouldn't have been touched until something to equal it was found.' When a Roman ship, which had lain in the mud near the Thames for 1900 years, looked like being destroyed during the same rebuilding, he turned up to help with the volunteer digging which saved the ship for posterity. He said at the time, 'We should save it. Remember, one

day they'll pull you and me down to build a block of flats.'
A few years after, his home in Finchley was pulled down
by developers.

Now he lives in a turreted home with leaded glass windows, which looks more like a mediaeval church than a
house, in the gentry's ghetto of Hadley Wood, surrounded
by the hunt masters and retired colonels he has satirized
so succinctly in his scripts. He joined in a World Day for
Animals march to Downing Street to urge official action
against hare coursing, otter hunting, and vivisection. When
American artist Newton Harrison announced plans to kill
lobsters, catfish, and shrimps by electrocution, he took a
hammer and smashed a window at the West End gallery
where the exhibition of ritual slaughter was to be held. In
Dublin, he gave a serious address to a conference on pollution. He said, 'One day I suddenly realized how much there
was to do. The conserving of the standards of architecture
and beauty, helping people and animals who are suffering.
You wouldn't believe how much cruelty there is to animals
in the manufacture of women's cosmetics. Manufacturers
test perfume by spraying it into a rabbit's eyes. If the rabbit goes
blind, the perfume is too strong for human use. Imagine that!'

The number of societies he backs are legion. 'I send them
all a bit of money. This is the way I can help.' When he is
not working, his pet charities and conservation projects take
up all his time. He has given free concerts to help save the
West Pier at Brighton, another Victorian masterpiece quaking under the threat of the demolition hammer, and charity
shows for battered wives. But his most celebrated cause saw
him in the role of Pixie Restorer to the Crown, when he
spent two years of his spare time renovating the carvings of
fairy figures on the Elfin Oak in Kensington Gardens, the
800-year-old oak which the wood carver Ivor Innes sculpted
into a glory of fantasy-land and woodland creatures. Milligan
noticed that many of the seventy carved figures were falling
to pieces and, after badgering the Ministry of Public Buildings and Works for over a year, he was allowed to work on
the tree. It had dry rot, damp rot, woodworm, and the death

watch beetle, and the figures – the elves, the pixies, the rabbits, the fox, and the birds – had almost rotted away. 'Nobody seemed to want to do anything about it. You see, there wasn't any profit in it, except, perhaps, to give some pleasure and a sense of wonder to a passing child. Money! That's all that interests people nowadays.' He decided to do the restoration himself, using his own cash and time.

Once, as he was working away one cold winter's day – behind the screens kindly put up by the Ministry of Works – a woman appeared at the foot of the ladder and asked, 'When are you going to get this bleedin' tree finished?'

Milligan said courteously, 'I'm doing my best.'

'Well, get a bleedin' move on,' she said. 'What a cheek, keeping the tree locked away from us like this.'

Her words infuriated him so much that he felt he could not face going on to a stage and trying to make an audience laugh. He added, equally sadly, 'While I was working on it, I knew it would be vandalized. It was, and I was heart-broken. But I will go back and work on it again, and hope the vandalism will be less next time.'

He has had other stays in psychiatric wards since his first traumatic breakdown. He tries to avoid the strains, because he realizes the depression, migraine, and black moods brought on by overwork make him a difficult person to live with. But he can't stop himself being an incessant worker, and can be seen wandering around scratching notes on a pad which he always carries with him. Said his wife Paddy with a shrug and a bright smile, 'When he's working on a project, he's in a world of his own and no one else is welcome there. Even I have to communicate with him by letter.' Spike recalls that first breakdown, 'I don't want it to happen again. And I don't want my second marriage to break up, because it's a good marriage. I'm much more aware now. I won't let them screw me up again. Sometimes when it gets on top of me, I just take a whole pile of letters and throw them away rather than answer them. I hate doing it, but I have to. It's the only way.'

Though Spike can laugh and joke for a show, the recurring

nervous depressions still make his own life far from amusing. 'Sometimes they last for a week, sometimes a month,' he said. 'I can remember what happiness was like and I know how to copy it, but I can't feel it. The tortuous part is having to go on with everyday life when you don't feel like talking to people. When I get like this, I spend a lot of time on my own. I don't want to inflict my illness on my family. They are all I live for, really. Mind you, it all began to get better when I met Paddy. If I didn't have my wife, I think I'd pack it all in.'

And despite the fact that he lives in such a wealthy and fashionable area, Spike insists, 'I still think I'm working class. I travel on the tube and always get a cheap return. You can't shake off the way you were brought up. When I spend money now, I feel my mother's breath on my back.'

When he is not working, he spends his time at home drawing, composing music, and polishing old brass and silver. They all offer temporary tranquillity. One day he envisages disappearing to live in the bush in Australia, in order to get away from his biggest enemy, the Inland Revenue. 'Dealing with taxes eats away my life,' he said. 'I work four months of every year filling up forms for the Government. Once when the Inspector of Taxes sent me a form I wrote a rude word across it and sent it back with a note saying: "Dear Sir, I am always filling up forms for you. Would you like to fill one up for me?"' Whereupon he enclosed a form he had drawn up with spaces for the Inspector to fill in his surname, Christian names, date of birth, parents' dates of birth ... There was no reply, but Milligan didn't really expect one. But he will continue to prick the balloons of pomposity with undiminished zeal and tilt at the complacent bureaucrats with the lance of comedy.

Millions of words have been written about Milligan and he has contributed a fair chunk himself, but as an individual he still remains an enigma. Like his own quest for perfection any attempt to define his personality is doomed to failure; it is as counter-productive as poking your finger into a glass of water.

76

'Don't deride the picture of the sad man inside the clown trying to get out,' he once said. 'The business about a clown being happy on stage and sad off is not just a myth. I have known that caricature to be me.'

It is an echo of the words he used when writing about his stage debut in the childhood Christmas Play. Perhaps it is as simple as that.

Chapter Five

SECOMBE – HAPPY CLOWN

None of Harry Secombe's countless fans and friends are at all surprised to learn that the favourite role of the hundreds he has played is Mr Pickwick, the roly-poly, bald-headed, myopic purveyor of 'If I Ruled the World' dreams. Quite apart from the generous proportions they have in common, there is a striking character resemblance between Dickens's fictional hero and the real, live bubbling boy from Swansea. They are both a little larger than life, accident-prone, incurable optimists, and lovers of their fellow beings. Harry explains his affection this way: 'I admire Pickwick's character ... a clown and buffoon with humanity and compassion in him.' It's the kind of thing people repeatedly say of Secombe. If he could wave some magic wand and become monarch of the universe the sentiments of the song he made famous really would come true. Every day *would* be the first day of spring.

The world of show business is not renowned for the depth of its sincerity. Everyone may be *darling* in public but there is a lot of envy, backbiting and character assassination in private. However, no one has ever been heard to say a bad thing about Harry Secombe. In 1971 the leading figures in the theatrical profession held a West End lunch – or 'love-in' as one writer described it – to honour his twenty-five years as an entertainer. He was hailed as 'the best loved figure in the business', and there wasn't a voice raised in disagreement in that narcissistic community. Secombe really doesn't have an enemy. Even his friends, Milligan and Sellers, who have at times tempered their praise of each other with outspoken criticism, have nothing but genuine admiration and affection for the heavyweight of the trio. His talent is as big as his waistline, and if he withdrew his cash from the bank tomorrow it could precipitate a City crash, yet he has remained a modest, uncomplicated man who is humbly grateful at being fortunate enough to do the thing he most enjoys – making people laugh.

His brother Fred Secombe, the vicar of Hanwell, a shortish, plump man with twinkling eyes, said at the Rectory in Church Road: 'Harry is tremendously loyal, sometimes loyal to the extent of being exploited. He would never renege or turn his back on anybody. He has a lot of fellow feeling, if I can put it that way, and a regard for the less fortunate which is truly genuine. He's not the sort who works for others in order to pave his way to heaven. People tell me, "Your brother is so lovable", and in show business, it is not often that you find people who call their fellow artists lovable. I agree with them. He is. He is a strong family man. He had a great regard for our father and mother and has very strong ties with my sister and myself. Also, he will listen to advice, even if he doesn't act on it. But listen he will.'

At the time of the anniversary luncheon James Green, the *Evening News* columnist, wrote a half-page tribute to Secombe in which he described him as 'The People's Pagliacci', but it was a description that was way off target. There is no broken hearted clown lurking behind that maniacal giggle. Secombe is a truly happy man. Off stage he is exactly the same person as he is on stage. 'I've been blessed with so much good fortune in my life, so much love and so much happiness – the very least I can do is spread some of it around,' he says.

One of his favourite quotations is from Frederick Langbridge's 'Cluster of Quiet Thoughts':

> *Two men look out through the same bars:*
> *One sees the mud, and one the stars.*

It sums up perfectly his attitude to life. He never sees the dark side of the moon and all clouds are silver-coated. Unlike Sellers and Milligan, when he looks back over his shoulder to the past it isn't with dislike or bitterness, it is with a sense of wonderment that life could have been so rich and full. Yet it hasn't been roses, roses all the way. He has taken a lot of hard knocks and there were times in his childhood when the going was really tough, especially in the depressed Twenties and Thirties. But what his family lacked in material possessions it made up for with an abundance of love. 'Ours was a typical Welsh family, close-knit, matriarchal; for the child a buttress of warmth and affection, with someone always there, if you fell down, to pick you up and kiss you better,' he recalled.

Harry Donald Secombe was born on 8th September, 1921, in a council house in Dan-y-Craig Terrace in the dock area of Swansea. The small house was shared with another family and the Secombes occupied two bedrooms upstairs and had the use of a parlour downstairs. His father was a clerk with a wholesale grocery firm and his mother was a hardworking woman who still found time to share the problems of her neighbours in her capacity as unofficial unpaid district nurse. They already had one son, Fred, aged $2\frac{1}{2}$ when Harry arrived, and three years later they had a daughter Carol. Their terraced home was overcrowded before she was born but, being a girl, Carol really complicated the sleeping arrangements. Fortunately the Secombes were given a whole council house to themselves in St Ledger Crescent where Harry, used to not being allowed into certain parts of the shared house, had to be assured that he wasn't trespassing if he used all the rooms. The terrace was four-sided and all the windows looked down on a small open space affectionately known as The Patch, so mothers could keep a watchful eye on their youngsters at play.

For the imaginative Harry that uneven square became a wonderland. In summer it became Lords for the cricket-mad boy, and with three stumps, no bails and an empty tin can to mark the bowler's crease, he became his hero, Harold

Larwood, the fast bowler whose phenomenal speed earned him the nickname 'Murder on tiptoe'. Said Fred, who has faced up to his thunderbolts: 'He's still quite good at cricket, too. As a lad he was the demon bowler of the local gang. He never allowed the ball to hit the ground, he simply concentrated at decapitating the kid with the bat. He takes a terrific run: still does, and it's pretty frightening when you see this short-sighted seventeen-stoner belting towards you. He enjoys cricket, and loves playing in the various charity matches. He can hit a ball a very long way when he connects properly – just as he can with a golf ball. He's been known to drive over three hundred yards. With the cricket bat, he's not in there to play strokes, but to see if he can whack the ball out of sight. Harry also loves the company of cricketers. Of course, that's where his interest with the Lords Taverners lies.'

On other occasions The Patch became the African bush where whitehunter Secombe pursued imaginary lions, while a blanket held up with broomsticks became an explorer's tent. There was no shortage of playmates on the estate, and they went fishing for tiddlers in nearby streams, explored the coves and bays of the nearby Gower Peninsular, and when the vigilant mothers relaxed their observation at their window vantage points they played games that established beyond doubt that little boys were different from little girls. 'The Patch remains in my mind and heart as a happy oasis from which I sometimes feel I have merely ventured,' he recalled more than forty years later.

His elder brother Fred shared many of his boyhood exploits, one of which particularly enraged Mrs Secombe. The local barber, to stimulate business, put a sign in his window offering to cut anyone's hair in the style of their favourite film star. Harry who spent much of his time day dreaming about his celluloid idols was dared by Fred to go in and accept the challenge. Harry did so but his cheekiness ended disastrously. When the barber asked him the name of his favourite star he cheekily replied, 'Rin Tin Tin'. 'Dai the hair' obliged by picking up his clippers and turning Harry into a Yul Brynner, and for weeks he had to wear his cap in class until his hair grew to a respectable length.

The docks with their towering cranes, the constant hoot of sirens of ships heading for, or returning from, distant lands, naturally played an influential part in his childhood. He would stand for hours on the quayside and watch the ships, and dream of the faraway places that were just patches in his school atlas. But dominating it all was the tall spire of St Thomas's Church with its four clock faces and eight gilt-covered hands looking like accusing fingers, which effectively ruled out any plausible excuse for being late for dinner. It was St Thomas's which was instrumental in moulding the future life of Secombe, for apart from singing in the choir and looking like a well scrubbed cherub in his cassock and white surplice, it was there that he made his stage debut.

While there was no great family show business tradition as there was with Sellers, there was a real enthusiasm for amateur shows. Harry's mother and father had first met when taking part in a local show, and at a time when money needed to be counted twice the family became adept at providing home entertainment. After Sunday evening service it became an established routine for the Secombe tribe to descend in force on a grandmother who lived in Jersey Terrace, and there they would gather round the piano for a singsong. Harry the choirboy was encouraged to sing, but he was so shy that at first he would only do so from the privvy in the garden.

Said brother Fred: 'Of course, Harry's great place for singing was out in the *ty bach* (loo to you). He used to sit and sing there for hours. He was on song when he sat down. I put this on the sleeve of one of Harry's records. They asked me to write about Harry's love of hymn singing, you see, and I said he was at his best when in the smallest room in the house. He likes church anthems too. We still sing Lead Me Lord now. It's a beautiful Wesley anthem. But Abide With Me is his favourite hymn.'

Gradually his mother persuaded him to do his impressions of local tradesmen and Harry discovered that he could overcome his inherent shyness when – like Sellers – he impersonated someone else. It provided him with a kind of protective mask. When he was eleven he gained a scholarship to Dynevor Secondary School where he established himself as the class wit. When asked to define satire he reduced his classmates to hysterical laughter by replying, 'A precious stone, sir.' His range of impersonations had also broadened to include the masters, and a couple of well-known radio comics.

But as an entertainer in the family's eyes he was really no great discovery; sister Carol had the *real* talent and Harry had to be satisfied with the role of stooge in the act she devised for a church social. Later he was permitted by the vicar to do a solo turn, and the diminutive Secombe did impersonations of Stanley Holloway, Stainless Stephen and Sandy Powell, and the Hollywood veteran Lionel Barrymore. Harry discovered he could shut out the audience, the mere sight of which transfixed him with stage fright, by simply removing his glasses. (It's something he still does.) The audience then dissolved into a vast warm thing he could wallow in. One day he threatens to write a thesis on comedy and myopia – so many comedians wear glasses – Max Bygraves, Peter Sellers, Eric Morecambe, Roy Castle, the late Jack Benny, to mention just a handful.

The Rev. Secombe recalls those childhood days: 'If anybody came to the house who was a bit of a character, Harry would do a great impression of him – or her – as soon as they had left. He has a gift of mimicry, and he's full of mischief. By comparison, I tended to be a bit of a prig in some ways. Harry just let things sail over his head. When I was head prefect, he would often come late to school. He'd come to the late door, and blithely rely on me getting him off punishment. The little blighter used to use that trick a bit too often.

'Harry was what I would call an off-and-on choirboy. A reluctant choirboy, you might say. He was good, mind you, and had a fine voice. He also gave a marvellous impersonation of the vicar's wife, or the vicaress, as we used to call her. Occasionally, he used to take her off in the middle of a hymn, much to the delight of the other boys, and the complete collapse of the choir. Harry often mitched from choir practice. He'd start out for the church, and never get there. He wasn't at all perturbed, whereas I never had a late mark throughout my schooldays, as far as I can remember, and was already about twenty-five miles towards heaven. He was always in mischief. He broke his glasses twice, I remember, and my mother would get so annoyed with him. But Harry would turn on the old charm, and she'd be giggling the next minute. He would get away with murder like that – things which I wouldn't dare contemplate.'

The poor eyesight which has afflicted him most of his life came about in an odd way. As a small child he was not particularly healthy, and apart from the normal run of children's complaints he suffered from scarlet fever, jaundice and an obscure tropical disease which the doctors suspected he had picked up off a banana boat in the harbour. When he returned to school after one spell in hospital he found the writing on the blackboard blurred and unreadable. He has needed glasses ever since.

His brother recalls: 'When Harry first went to school he wouldn't go into a class with lads of his own age, but insisted on sitting next to me in my class. He was very shy and had little confidence in himself. But after a couple of weeks, he got used to doing without big brother, and went into the normal infants class. I don't know whether this has any psychological significance, but this same lack of confidence was evident when he was very young, and first started to do a little entertaining. We used to have a concert every so often at the Band of Hope, and I can remember that Harry was going to give a few impressions at one of them. He was very good at imitating everybody, including his teachers. He started with Ronald Colman, and worked his way up. Harry was marvellous when he was within the family circle, but as soon as he got on the stage he was ill at ease, and extremely nervous. I remember my father saying "He'll never be able to do anything with that act, he just hasn't got the confidence." '

Harry, who has become an author of considerable distinction, writes about his childhood with such a freshness and originality that he creates word pictures that conjure up the smells, sounds, and sheer zest for living of those Swansea days. The people come alive, and the smell of fish and chips, freshly cooked cockles, and Laverbread made from seaweed are wonderfully evoked. He frequently returns to his home town, but unlike Sellers he is not questing or searching for anything. As he said recently in an article for the *Sunday Times Magazine*: 'I shall always love Swansea for two things. First for a happy childhood and second for providing me with a wife. I have never really left Swansea, I have taken it with me.'

He liked school and was far from being a dullard. He loved reading and developed a lasting passion for poetry. But he was a far from reluctant leaver. In those times every family was grateful for an extra breadwinner. Even at that green and salad stage he had an eye for figures, but certainly no head for them. Again brother Fred: 'Harry was very good at English, and always got good marks, but, like all the Secombes, he was appalling at science and maths. In geometry, he had the distinction of getting nought out of a hundred when he sat his Central Welsh Board examination – the equivalent of Matriculation in England. When the results were announced, his master said: "We have a genius in the form. Secombe, COME OUT HERE!" Apparently, he was the first boy in the history of the school to get a nought.'

Coal was still the life blood of Wales, and although Harry did not don a helmet and hew the black diamonds from a coal seam with a pickaxe, he went to work in the pay office of a local colliery. There he engaged in a lucrative if illegal racket for making an extra few pence pocket money. Unlike Milligan, whose first and only venture into skulduggery was in order to buy a much desired trumpet, Harry's was strictly mercenary. As the most junior member of the staff he was expected to make the tea and he found that, by charging a penny a cup, he was a few pence in at the end of the week. Some of the more senior members, obviously concerned with rank and status, expressed a liking for a more expensive and aromatic brand of tea, so Harry used to fill an empty canister of a more snobbish brew with a cheaper blend, and increase his profit margin even more. In no time at all his services as tea brewer *par excellence* were in demand in other departments, and by throwing in (for free) a liberal helping of broken biscuits he was able to expand his takings still further. But the career of the budding Lipton was brought to an abrupt halt. Chamberlain had come back from Munich proudly proclaiming that his heart-to-heart talks with Hitler had resulted in 'peace in our time', and quoting Shakespeare's 'from out this nettle danger we pluck this flower, safety', but no one really believed that the war could be put off much longer. Secombe like many other of the colliery's pen pushers joined the Territorial Army, not so much in a burst of patriotic fervour, but simply because they had all been led to believe that Terriers under twenty-one would not be liable for conscription, which everyone knew was just around the corner. At seventeen the poetry-loving Secombe was not in a Rupert Brooke frame of mind; he didn't relish the idea of a grave in some far foreign field that was for ever Wales. But conscience must have stricken him, for soon afterwards he headed straight for the nearest recruiting centre, added two years to his age, and joined the army. While he was on manoeuvres, the war that everyone had confidently predicted, broke out. Gunner Secombe of 321 Battery, official number 924378, armed with Palgraves Golden Treasury, and a rather antiquated Lee Enfield .303 rifle, stood by to repel the Germans. At a Staffordshire camp where they were sleeping under canvas Secombe experienced gunfire for the first time when he accidentally pulled the trigger of his loaded rifle and sent a bullet crashing into the earth a few inches away from a sleeping comrade who, in his panic, dived into a nearby lake breaking a big toe.

The rifle shot made everyone fear that the invasion had started, and a breathless, revolver-brandishing major shouted a rousing 'Come on lads', and went into action – only to find a rather penitent Secombe holding on to a smoking Lee

Enfield. The major shrugged and dismissed the ready-to-die-in-battle rookies. 'It's all right,' he said resignedly, 'it's only that idiot Secombe.'

He wasn't the only officer to refer to Secombe in such derogatory terms. It was a phrase repeated on various battle-fields where Harry modestly claimed to have played 'walk on' parts.

Harry had started the war with a chaotic situation which was repeatedly, if unintentionally, to mirror the remainder of his service career. Comic catastrophies were never far away from the short-sighted pongo, who discovered that the battlefield was littered with banana skins. Like his friend, Milligan, how-ever, he was never really able to talk or write about the war in all its grim blood-letting aspects. He had to cloud the horror behind the amusing anecdote, or a story of self-denigration. It was rather like a small boy who pulls the sheets over his head to shut out the bogy man. But in a more serious moment, when he was once asked if he had had a good war, he snapped abrasively that only an arms manu-facturer could have a *good* war.

His unit developed into a crack fighting outfit and was shipped to Algiers as part of the British First Army. There he became involved with that advance-retreat series of con-frontations with the Germans that hallmarked the African campaign. Once, during a hard fighting drive towards Tunisia, they were halted at a place called Tebourba where they ran out of ammunition, supplies, and overhead support, and re-ceived a humiliating clobbering.

It was soon after this that the classic encounter took place which – while not materially affecting the course of the war – had a profound effect on the future of British comedy. He met Milligan in the howitzer fiasco already mentioned. From then on, as Harry puts it, he and Milligan 'played walk on parts in battles', and kept up the morale of their comrades in arms.

One incident Secombe is never allowed to forget was his arrest of the high ranking German officer at a small outpost called Medjez-el-Bab. In the half light and with his unreliable eyesight, Secombe mistook a paratrooper's helmet for a German one and arrested Randolph Churchill, the son of Winston the Prime Minister. On another occasion, this time during the invasion of Sicily, he inadvertently played the role of the cool, nerveless bomb-disposal man, and no one, despite his fervent protestations that he was a reluctant hero, would accept that he hadn't risked life and limb to save a small village from extermination.

It happened when he and a pal were out on a reconnaissance patrol seeking a suitable spot on which to site a battery of 25-pounder guns. They suddenly arrived at a small near-deserted village which had clearly been the target of a recent air assault. Dead donkeys lay in the streets and the locals seemed to have fled. Suddenly they spotted a beautiful peasant girl standing at the fountain in the village square, and their minds automatically turned to thoughts of a glass of the local plonk. In spaghetti Italian they asked her where they could find some vino, and they were most encouraged when she beckoned them towards her house. They climbed the stairs with breathless anticipation, for by now Secombe and his pal were convinced that it was not only their thirst that was about to be satisfied. Then, when the girl nervously opened the bedroom door, they saw to their horror an un-exploded five hundred pounder American Air Force bomb the size of a well-fed pig nestling snugly on the bed, which only seconds earlier had conjured up transports of delight. A cursory, and not too close inspection, convinced Secombe that the bomb was harmless and, fortified with a couple of glasses of head-reeling vino, he and his friend wheeled the bed out of the house, down the hill into the open space outside the village. As the bed careered crazily down the steep incline, Secombe bellowed a theatrical 'Down everybody'. It was just as well for the bomb exploded with a deafening crump that shattered the few remaining undamaged windows in the village.

The grateful villagers produced bottles of wine from hidden sources, and invited Secombe and his pal to imbibe as deeply and as frequently as they wished. It was an abortive binge, for minutes later their officer arrived on the scene, bucolic with rage at finding his scouts sitting in the village square, guzzling the booze. 'We're moving on in ten minutes and here you are swilling wine with the ruddy natives. Get in the jeep before I shoot the whole damned lot of you,' he shouted. No one mentioned the bomb.

But war was like that for the accident-prone Secombe. Apart from the pontoon bridge fiasco he also broke his glasses and was sent to hospital labelled 'walking wounded'. There a confusion over labels ended up with him being given VIP treatment, while the poor unfortunate soldier with dysentery, who was thought to have suffered nothing worse than a broken spectacle frame, was ordered to fill sandbags and dig fortification ditches.

In between the all-too-few periods of relaxation, Secombe entertained his comrades at improvised regimental and divisional concerts, and when the shooting finally stopped he joined the Central Pool of Artists, that nursery for so many entertainers who later became big stars. As has already been stated he teamed up with Milligan and other aspiring stars, among them Alfred Marks, Norman Vaughan and Nigel Patrick. The troops who had seen almost uninterrupted action for months, even years, were at a loose end, and diversion was the keynote. Quantity, not quality, was the order of the day. One of the shows in which he figured with Milligan was called 'Over the Page', and it toured all over Italy, and even got as far as Austria. It was an ideal laboratory for Secombe and Milligan to carry out their experiments in comedy, and as he has so often remarked it laid the foundation stones for The Goons.

Briefly he touched the hem of stardom: he operated the spotlight for Gracie Fields when she gave an army concert in Italy. Not only was he honoured but he learned a valuable lesson which has stayed with him throughout his career. As he watched Gracie he realized that an audience puts its idols on pedestals, and in return expects conduct in keeping with that honour. 'If you're a revered person you have a sort of responsibility.'

(Many years later when he was a star himself and running to catch a train, with a suitcase in each hand and one under his arm, he was stopped on the platform by an autograph hunter. With only seconds to spare he pantingly asked the fan to drop him a line at the BBC and he would send off a signed picture – which he did.)

When he was running short of laughter-raising material Harry resorted to singing the odd song but he never envisaged himself as a singer of any import. His forte was the belly laugh. But it was a shaving mishap which first gave him the idea for a sketch which turned out to be the turning point in his life. It provided him with the material which was to be the vehicle to carry him into the professional ranks, and eventual stardom. While he was lathering his chin with his service issue brush, prior to removing the stubble with his service issue razor, he inadvertently smeared soap over his glasses and into his eyes. It suddenly occurred to him that there was the making of a good comedy routine on how various people shave. With his gift for mimicry there seemed no end to the changes he could ring. He spent hours standing in front of the mirror perfecting the sketch, and by the time he was satisfied with it, he had a chin that was as red and sore as a baboon's backside. Andy Gray, the entertainments writer for the service paper *First Army News*, was immensely impressed, and told Secombe he had the kernel of a first class act. 'When you come out of the army, let me know and I'll try to get you started in show business,' he promised.

Six and a half years after his enlistment Harry Secombe was demobbed as a Lance Bombardier, with a new suit, a pork pie hat he had purchased from a hard-up officer, and £80 gratuity in crispy new notes. He was twenty-three, lean as a Welsh whippet and weighed just under nine stone. And romance had entered his life on a once and forever basis.

At a Swansea Saturday night hop on Mumbles Pier, he had met an attractive young girl named Myra Atherton who had worked in a munitions factory during the war. Secombe had at first tried to impress her by masquerading as a

Canadian soldier, but when she cut him down to size with a terse Welsh rejoinder that adequately conveyed her opinion of Swansea-born cowboys, he reverted to his natural self and got her to agree to a cinema date. But when the time came to meet the attractive brunette he couldn't quite remember what she looked like, so he hid himself behind a post and kept observation. The appointed time came and went and the minutes ticked by, and when there was still no sign of Myra he was convinced he had been stood up. Then, just as he was about to leave for a consoling pint she emerged from behind another pillar. She too had been hiding in order to get a good look at her date before committing herself.

Secombe decided that she was the girl he wanted to marry. But first there was a future to think about. He knew in his heart that he wanted to make entertainment his career, but he seriously doubted whether he had the ability or confidence to make a success of it. Playing to receptive army audiences, who were more sympathetic to amateurs than they were to established artists, was one thing, but what kind of reception could he expect from people who had paid hard-earned cash at the box office? The nagging doubts were understandable but a trifle premature; no one was rushing forward to offer engagements and the horizon looked very bleak indeed.

It was during a job search through London's theatreland in the summer of 1946 that Harry bumped into Gray again, and he suggested that the Welshman should try to get an audition at the Windmill Theatre, that launching pad for so many young ex-service comedians. Harry went home to Wales, wrote a letter to the theatre's owner, sat back and awaited a reply. It came quite promptly and asked him to present himself at the stage door at 9.30 a.m. He packed his shaving brush, mug and soap stick, caught the train to London and spent the night with relatives at Romford. He got up at the crack of dawn, ate a far-from-hearty breakfast, then walked to the nearest bus stop, giving himself a good three hours to make the ten-mile odd journey to Soho. All he had was his demob suit, a few pounds in his Post Office book, and a few words of home-spun philosophy once given to him by his father: 'Judge a man by the way he treats people who can do nothing for him.' He was also fortified with a lot of encouragement from Myra, who had no qualms about his ability. She was already his staunchest fan, and she has remained so with unswerving loyalty.

Thirty years later his brother expanded on that seeming lack of confidence: 'There are depths in Harry which people sometimes don't realize. He's got a sense of vocation, and dedication. I think this is partly religious in a sense. We went for a walk one day, not long after he had left the army, and he asked me if I thought it was possible to have a vocation to be a comedian. Could you possibly call it a vocation? he wanted to know, and I remember reassuring him that you certainly could. I said that people were called to do all kinds of things in life, and I said that to be a good comedian was an important job. Surely to be able to make people laugh, is one of the finest gifts man can have.'

There is no more dreary place than the West End of London in the early morning. The pavements are littered with the remnants of the previous night's revels, and the only people up and about are those homeless souls who find meagre warmth and comfort sleeping in the doorways, with newspapers for sheets, or huddling under the hot-air vents of a deserted office block. Secombe had two hours to kill when he arrived at Piccadilly, and he wandered aimlessly round the theatres looking at the famous names in unlit lights above the foyers, and at the glossy studio portraits in glass-fronted show cases. Eventually he found himself outside the Windmill, looking at the celebrated roll of honour which listed all the people who had started there and made the big time. There was no similar board listing the countless number of young men and women who had tried, not made it and vanished into obscurity. The Windmill could also be a graveyard, and Secombe wondered into which category he would land. The theatre was locked and bolted, so he whiled away a little more time drinking an unwanted cup of coffee in one of those faceless little cafes which, like the Windmill, never seem to close. With a stomach full of butterflies that felt like giant bats, he straightened his shoulders and headed for the stage door; if he flopped he would accept defeat gracefully and head home for the safety and security and unutterable boredom of life as a clerk at Baldwin's Colliery.

Secombe was not the only one taking a professional audition for the first time; there were singers with vocal chords paralysed with nerves, magicians with fumbling fingers, jugglers and fellow comics. Secombe unpacked his handful of props and joined the queue. His fast-waning confidence was eroded even more when he was told to be sure to be in the wings on time, as some of the acts didn't last long. They were quickly terminated by a chilly 'Thank you' kiss-of-death. Harry got off to an inauspicious start, for as he was standing in the wings lathering his chin, the stage manager remarked icily, 'You should have shaved before you came here.' When Harry explained that it was all part of his act, he received an indifferent shrug in response, and the man walked away shaking his head in a manner that suggested he thought the aspiring comedian was a trifle nutty.

Two turns ahead of Secombe was a young man with a lop-sided smile who wasn't much taller than a schoolboy. His forte was to do a musical turn, crack a few jokes, then fall flat on his face, laughing helplessly. He had barely started his routine when a voice as cold as charity came floating up from the darkened auditorium: 'Thank you.' The young fall-about comic picked himself up, dredged a smile that hid his disappointment, and walked off. He knew his name wouldn't make the honours board outside. He did, however, make it big elsewhere. His name was Norman Wisdom, and his Chaplin-esque humour was to make him a world-famous star.

Next on was a magician whose legerdemain prompted the same two chilly words, 'Thank you', when he was barely through his first trick.

With knocking knees Secombe took the stage to a piano accompaniment of 'I'm Just Wild About Harry'. His signature tune hadn't unduly impressed anyone by its originality. Undeterred he went into his routine with his shaving mug, brush and razor reposing on the top of a borrowed card table, demonstrating how various kinds of people carried out that vital morning ritual. All the time his ears were waiting to hear the death knell from the stalls. He got through the shaving bit without hearing a word, then he ended his turn with a take-off of those silver screen idols Jeannette Mac-donald and Nelson Eddy singing a duet. Secombe's voice switched from tenor to soprano with startling ease as he sang his way through the syrupy lyrics of 'Sweetheart', and for the parts where they had to sing together he broke into a high pitched Swiss yodel. He finished and peered hopefully into the seats below, but without his glasses he couldn't see a thing. Suddenly the voice of the theatre's owner, the legendary Vivian Van Damn, called out matter-of-factly, 'All right, come and see me upstairs in my office.'

In the small but famous office where so many people had taken the first step up the ladder of success, the maestro asked, 'How much do you want?' Secombe recalled some advice he had received from Norman Vaughan on how to reply if that question was ever put – ask for double you expect to get then gradually come down. 'Twenty pounds a week,' said Harry, happily prepared to come down to the figure he would settle for, namely £10. Van Damn, never a word-waster, said, 'Right,' and instructed his secretary to draw up a contract. In a semi-trance Secombe signed, agreeing to do six shows a day, six days a week for a period of six weeks, commencing 17th October 1946, Carol's birthday.

It sounds like slave labour until one accepts that comedians were the last thing the all-male audience at the Windmill went to hear. They were just necessary time-fillers, slotted in while the girls went off to change for a new routine and get rid of the goose pimples. The men had simply come to gaze drooly-mouthed at the beautiful nudes. It seems all very tame stuff in this age of full-frontal nudity and strip clubs, for at the Windmill the girls were not allowed to move, and ostrich feather fans discreetly covered their pubic region. Nevertheless there were always long queues to get into the theatre, whose famous wartime motto 'We Never Closed' had been vulgarized into 'We never clothed'. Even so an act had to be good to survive, for when the comics were on, the men in grubby raincoats turned the theatre into a Grand National course, clambering over the backs of seats to get nearer to the stage in readiness for the real stuff.

Secombe had yet to discover that and, floating on air, he went to the nearest post office and sent two telegrams – one to his mother, the other to Myra: 'Booked at Windmill at Twenty Pounds a Week Love Harry'.

Shaving six times a day played hell with Secombe's complexion; his pores became so impregnated with soap that whenever he was caught in the rain his face disappeared under a beard of lather. He looked like the Ancient Mariner. It was an exhausting six weeks but invaluable training for the beginner; it provided experience in assessing the mood of an audience, and at the end Secombe was confident that no matter where he appeared afterwards, he would never meet such a hostile or resentful one. (He happened to be wrong on that score.)

During his spell at the Windmill he met many up-and-coming artists, among them Michael Bentine, with whom he struck up a close and lasting friendship. Bentine, one of the most talented and original comics ever to win over a Windmill audience, shared Harry's ambition to lift British humour out of the rut it had been stuck in for so long. Secombe was living in digs in Kilburn, a far-from-fashionable part of London, and in the evenings he would go to Allen's Club in Great Windmill Street where, with Bentine and other entertainers, they talked into the early hours about their ideas on comedy. Milligan soon joined them and later Sellers began to drop in. Shortly afterwards The Grafton Arms became the experimental base for their own unique brand of humour, with Bentine and Milligan being the main ideas men.

But the euphoria of the first engagement at the Windmill soon wore off; Secombe discovered that permanent success didn't come that easily. Once, when sharing digs with Milligan in Earls Court, they were both so short of cash they had to do a 'moonlight flit'. A few television engagements followed, plus the odd cabaret date, and a not-too-frequent booking in provincial theatres.

At the Clapham Grand a member of the audience expressed his dislike of Secombe's act by loosing off an air gun. While it didn't teach Secombe anything about the material, it instilled in him the importance of mobility. At the Finsbury Park Empire he blotted his copybook, and lost a future engagement, by appearing on stage wearing a dinner jacket and tweed trousers. He was so hard up that he only had one dress suit, and he had taken the pants to the dry cleaners intending to pick them up on the Monday morning. When he arrived at the shop he found to his horror that it was closed. He'd forgotten it was Bank Holiday Monday. An even worse catastrophe occurred at the Grand Theatre, Bolton, during the annual Wakes Week. There his act died the death. As he went through his shaving routine there wasn't a ripple of laughter from the stony-faced audience who sat tightly in their seats, their expressions conveying grim disapproval. When Secombe reached his 'Sweetheart' duet he felt as if there was an iron band clamped round his larynx like a garrotte. He managed to get through the number and finished with a piercing high note, and his hands thrown back in a gesture of surrender.

The audience came to life and he walked into the wings with the demoralizing sound of the slow hand clap echoing in his ears. He had been given the bird.

It happens at some time or another to every entertainer, but that knowledge didn't help Secombe. Utterly dejected he went to his dressing room, changed, then headed for the bar and a sedative. There, as he slumped over the bar, he heard mutterings and whisperings about the quality of his act. He tapped one of the moaners on the shoulder and told him in no uncertain manner how well his turn had gone down with the more sophisticated London audiences. Bolton, he said disparagingly, just wasn't ready for such stuff. It was a tactical error. The man happened to be the theatre owner, and promptly told Harry to catch the first train in the morning. 'You're not shaving in my bloody time,' he said.

rry caught the train, pausing only long enough to send now-famous telegram to Michael Bentine. It had been a rve wracking time but it revealed the strength of Secombe's character. He shrugged it off and came bouncing back like a rubber ball.

Secombe the incurable optimist was often down but never out. In his book, *Goon for Lunch*,* he summed up his attitude to a bad reception with these words, 'Then comes Monday and a wonderful first house, and the journey back to the digs through the smell of fish and chips and candy floss, and the sound of Tetley best bitter is a joyous one, because if they were like this tonight they're going to be sensational tomorrow night. And of course they never are ... but just wait until Wednesday.' And in the same book he wrote of the pleasure derived from cooking spaghetti on a gas ring in a kitchen where the paper was peeling off the walls; clubbing together to pay the rent and buy grub, and rushing out into the pouring rain in only his pants and vest, blowing off steam just at the sheer exhilaration of being alive.

Compare that with Sellers' loathing for digs and the smells that pervade them and you have the essential difference between the two friends. 'You know,' he once explained, 'we comedians have to develop a skin that's thick enough to take the knocks, the humiliations, the defeats and the flops. Because, let me tell you mate, this is a hard business. There's nothing more painful than a comedian getting out there on stage and no one laughing.'

He could have gone for the 'blue' joke and got cheap laughs, but he stubbornly resisted. As Fred put it: 'Harry would never use any blue material. Even today, if there is anything in a script which he thinks is slightly off, he is very reluctant to do it, and will more than likely ask for it to be taken out.'

In 1948 Secombe went back to St Thomas's Church in Swansea, the scene of so many happy childhood memories, to make Myra Atherton Mrs Secombe. He had proposed to her over tea and cakes in a small cafe in the town, and

* Published by Robson.

The young Milligan gives a fireside chat.

Above Even at his wedding Spike plays the fool. But what is that swine Seagoon telling the bride? *Below* Daughter Jane's christening.

Milligan is the most controversial Goon. *Above* He puts a hammer through a window in protest against experiments on live shellfish; *below* he leaves court after admitting shooting at a boy in his garden; *opposite* he campaigns for Beauty Without Cruelty.

Above With Eric Sykes in the TV show *Joke Factory*. *Below* Announcing the end of his long-running West End hit *Son of Oblomov*.

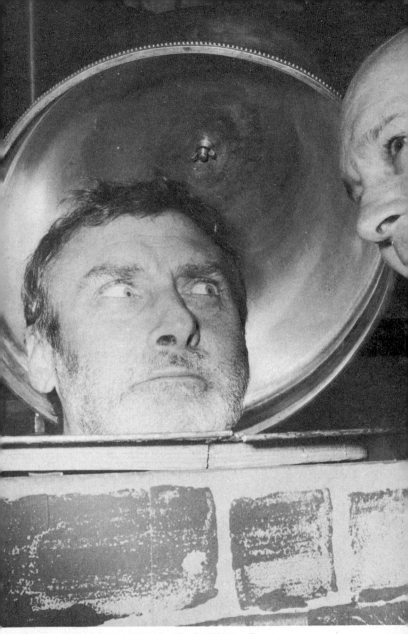

Spike's head served on a salver in *The Bed Sitting Room*.

The Ecclesiastical Sports — from BBC2's *Milligan in Autumn*.

Harry and Myra *above* on their wedding day and *below* with new-born Katy.

Mr and Mrs Secombe with Andrew and Jennifer: off on holiday.

Above A break in rehearsals for the 1958 Royal Variety Show: (from left) Max Bygraves, Bernard Bresslaw, Harry and Tony Hancock. *Below* In 1967 Secombe was back on the Royal show.

All those Royal Variety Shows went to Harry's head . . .

Above Harry's 25th anniversary in showbusiness. *Below* When he took the part of a plumber in *Schippel* he said: 'It's *not* a kitchen-sink drama . . .'

Harry at 50, still clowning. The hat is Katy's.

Mr Pickwick collects for Oxfam.

promised her that if she accepted him a life of champagne and caviar lay ahead. Well, she had accepted, but the promised life of luxury was as yet nowhere in sight. His friend Ronnie Bridges, who had played the piano for him at the Windmill, was seated at the organ. Harry's elder brother, 'Rev. Fred', conducted the service, which went without a hitch until the groom was asked to slip the ring on the bride's third finger. Harry, in a high state of nerves, put it on the wrong finger, but was fortunately rescued by Fred who muttered, 'On the other one, you nit.'

After a short honeymoon in Cornwall, Harry returned to digs in London and the pursuit of the promised champagne and caviar, while Myra went home to her family. The couple only managed to meet when Harry was 'resting'. Twenty-eight years later it is held up as the happiest marriage in show business. Said Myra, 'I can truthfully say we have one of the happiest marriages I know. There are not so many women – especially showbiz wives – who can say that and mean it, and I am humbly grateful that I can. He's a very considerate husband and father.'

Harry says, 'She's my Rock of Gibraltar...' and fearing he might be sounding mawkish, adds laughingly, 'and I'm one of the apes. I could go home tomorrow and say I'd lost everything and she'd say, "Never mind love. Let's put the kettle on and have a cup of tea." She gives me a sense of security, because of her own lovely quality of steadfastness. I am what I am because she is what she is.'

On occasions the larder was so bare that Myra and Harry had to sit down to a meal consisting of nothing but potatoes. Today they have everything they want, but it was slow in coming. For a time they lived in rented rooms which never seemed free of the smell of washed nappies drying on a clothes horse in front of the fire. Not that it ever worried or depressed him. What's love anyway? he'll ask, then answer, 'It's acceptance of things, dirty socks and soiled underpants and smells on the landings.'

Gradually the good times, which for so long had seemed a mirage, began to assume concrete proportions. Harry was in demand for radio shows and television appearances, and then came The Goon Shows. They were happy days for Ned of Wales, alias Ned Seagoon, but he refuses to read anything of real significance in the new style humour, although he realizes it was a tremendous step forward. 'For Peter and me it was just a giggle. We never analysed it. I suppose it was an oral cartoon. I read once that there were shades of Kafka, Ionesco and Dylan Thomas in it. Really it was just three blokes having a laugh, coupled with Spike's inventive genius.' Once when he was asked to define his role in The Goon Shows he said they needed a maypole to dance round, and that was him.

For Secombe those Sunday shows were a great safety valve, and when he turned up at the studio he always felt like a kid who had just been let out of school. He would burst on stage singing snatches from some Italian aria, while Sellers would be lying under the piano playing a set of bongo drums. Milligan would strike up, 'We'll Keep a Welcome' on the piano ... Then all hell would break loose. Shouts of 'It's Singo' or 'Hullo my capitain' filled the air. Someone would bellow, 'He's wearing a tenor's friend' (The Goons' description for a truss with a spike attached). Sometimes Sellers would cause a panic by phoning and saying he couldn't make it; then he would walk through the door with a wide grin on his face. He had called from his phone-installed car, parked outside. Harry would let rip with one of his celebrated raspberries and drop his trousers, making certain first that he hadn't forgotten to put on his underpants. Someone would shout 'Cobblers' in response to some ribald remark. Then after a read-through of the script, a lot of ad-libbing and alterations, plus a spell of head-standing, they would depart for a quick one in the pub next door.

They would return, passing the queue outside, which would yell some of the Goon snatches of conversation which had become catch phrases. Then, armed with a bottle of milk and a flask of brandy for a bracer during the musical interludes, they prepared for the actual recording.

It ended as crazily as it began with the three of them

signing autographs and exchanging pleasantries with the fans before heading home. Secombe couldn't wait for the week to pass for Sunday to come round again. He had really enjoyed every hilarious minute. 'Laughter is like air, the air we breathe, and I can't have enough of it,' he would say.

The longer the series ran the better they got. There was the 'Search in the Street of a Thousand Households', 'The Case of the Hairy Bus', 'The Phantom Head Shaver of Bexhill', 'The House of Teeth', 'The Affair of the Lone Banana' and countless other gems.

But all good things must come to an end, and after six long years the curtain came down on The Goon Shows. 'We didn't want to grind it to death,' said Harry.

The real fame that had so long eluded Secombe was now reality. He became a big name in his own right, and was more and more in demand as a stage personality, although he tended to get billed as 'The Golden voiced Goon'. For some considerable time he had been taking singing lessons from Manlio de Veroli, the famous Italian teacher who had established himself in London, and Secombe took his voice-rebuilding with great seriousness. No matter where he was appearing, he never missed a lesson, even if it meant travelling to London at the most ungodly hours. During the initial part of his career Secombe had considered his voice – although it had a two-and-a-half octave range – as simply an amusing vehicle to end his act. But once when he was singing 'Buddy Can you Spare a Dime', and at a time when he really meant it, he was told: 'Harry, you ought to sing a song right through without messing it about.' The advice came from Mai Jones, producer of Welsh Rarebit, a hit BBC radio show in which Harry appeared during the fifties. She scolded him roundly if his irrepressible sense of fun caused him to wreck a song he was singing, by crossing his eyes, or blowing a raspberry. And when she heard him sing Rodgers and Hart's evergreen hit 'Falling in Love with Love', Mai encouraged him to have his voice trained.

Manlio de Veroli, who had taught some of the world's finest opera singers, including Gigli, took the comic as a pupil, and literally rebuilt his voice. A hard taskmaster, he would keep Secombe singing one phrase for months before indicating that he was satisfied. The endless round of music halls had inevitably resulted in Harry acquiring a lot of bad vocal habits, and Veroli eliminated these with the ruthlessness of a surgeon removing a poisonous abscess. The singing lessons continued without interruption until 1961, when the elderly Italian died. Secombe's professional approach to singing gave rise to the myth that he was really torn between a career in opera and comedy, but Harry never had any delusions of grandeur. The vision of filling Covent Garden never really appealed to him. He was more than content to play the fool and then sing seriously. The long run of an operatic season appealed to him as little as the idea of singing Pagliacci for a living. He was a clown but there was nothing broken-hearted about him.

Says brother Fred: 'Manlio told me: "Your brother has a fine voice. It could be a great one, if only he'd give up all this clowning." I told him there wasn't the slightest hope of that, as Harry got so much out of making people laugh. Anyway, seriously, can you imagine Harry in Wagner?'

Secombe was now able to turn to Myra, stick his tongue out and say: 'I told you so.' The champagne and caviar had arrived. But Myra was always there to make sure that Harold Donald Secombe, the council estate boy from Swansea, didn't get big-headed, and kept his two feet firmly planted on the ground. When he returned home one night, full of justifiable self-importance, to announce that he was now in the £1,000 week category and was to top the bill at the Palladium, Myra told him to keep his voice down as the doctor was upstairs attending their young son Andrew, who had measles. And when the family doctor finally descended the stairs and wrote out a presciption on the kitchen table, Harry was promptly despatched to the chemist to collect it.

Throughout their long and happy married life Myra – she calls him Har and he calls her My – was always there to curb those giddy flights to the moon on the gossamer wings of stardom. No man was a star to his own family, she told him. He was just plain Dad. And once when he had landed a lucrative film part and was being treated like an oil-rich sheikh, and on the brink of being full of his own self-importance, Myra shoved an empty scuttle under his nose and said, 'Right, Gregory Peck. Get the coal in.' When he moved into the Top Ten in the hit parade, his children affectionately described him as being an idle pop, rather than a pop idol.

That healthy attitude is one of the reasons why Secombe has remained so natural and unaffected by material success. He is genuinely a family man, and that is not an image conjured up by cynical press agents. He really enjoys it. With all his money, there's nothing available on the market to replace it. He and his family have lived in the same big house in Cheam for more than twenty-five years, and when he gets home he likes to pull the door to and shut out the tinsel and trappings of show business life, put on an apron, and peel the spuds or help with the washing up.

Harry tends to dress casually and his one piece of self-indulgence is a chauffeur-driven Rolls with an HS 92 number plate – 'my initials and waistline'. But the driver is one of the family and, in any case, weighing in at $17\frac{1}{2}$ stone it's one of the few cars he can be comfortable in. He has, he admits, invested his money wisely. He has a seafront villa in Majorca with cool patios, and a Moorish fountain generously shaded by palm trees. One day he threatens to retire there and write. He also has a camera and a perfume shop. The Secombes have holidayed in the West Indies and Harry has been able to make those day dreams of safaris in Africa's game parks come true. If his waistline has grown over the years, his size in hats has remained the same.

'Those are the perks,' he says, 'but most of my life is spent in the theatre. You can't pull the big star stuff today. The days of the star leading an aloof existence are over; it was always a phoney. The important thing is to surround yourself with people you like, make yourself amenable, know them all, take an interest in everybody.'

They are not pious sentiments. Anyone who has worked

with Secombe will confirm that he never loses his temper or indulges in temperamental tantrums. If he thinks anyone in the show has a problem he takes the trouble to find out what it is and help to sort it out. It is the side the public doesn't see. And his generosity is legendary. But it's something he dislikes talking about. 'If the little I do is considered generous, it's a sorry indictment of our times. I'm only doing what my father would have done, or any average person.'

Said his brother: 'Harry is a very generous person, and has been very kind to us. He has helped a great many people in show business who have been down on their luck, and quite a few have taken advantage of him. If you are like he is, you are vulnerable. But there it is: that's the way he's made, and he'll never change. I remember he bought us a television so that we could see the Coronation. I was just starting then as a country parson, and we really appreciated it. He was so kind to our parents, too.'

But he'll talk as long as you will listen about cricket. One of the most valued things that fame and success have brought him is the repeated requests to play in charity cricket matches. He is a Lords Taverner and is like a dog with two tails when he leads a team of showbiz stars and Test cricketers out on to the field. Nothing gives him greater pleasure than to toss the ball to an England fast bowler and remark nonchalantly, 'See what you can do with that,' or tell Cowdrey to get padded up, he's in next.

It was his work for the Army Benevolent Fund which resulted in him being awarded the C.B.E., but much as he felt honoured he didn't do it for any tangible recognition. He derives untold delight from making others laugh and bringing a little sunshine into lives that have been deprived of it. He regularly entertains handicapped children, and he just cannot understand how anyone could be so heartless as to neglect or ignore them. After one concert he was so overwhelmed by their gratitude that he felt like weeping.

'And I realized that as long as I have the gift to entertain and make people forget some of their troubles, I have a responsibility to give as much of myself as I can. And there's a lot of me to go round!'

There's another reason for his incredible generosity, whether it's in cheque form, the offer of a job, or merely giving his talents free. Harry suffers from a deep feeling of guilt – guilt at being paid such large sums for doing what he loves.

Long before The Goons finished he was an established star, but it was during a family holiday in Barbados in Christmas 1961 that he hit upon an idea that was to rocket him into the international bracket. For a Christmas spectacular he had played the part of a Dickensian inn keeper, and his picture in period costume was on the front cover of *TV Times*. As Secombe looked at the photograph, the germ of an idea for a musical began to develop. His voice under Manlio's expert tuition had improved beyond measure, and Harry began thinking of a lavish stage musical in which he could blend his talents as a singer and comedian. The cover photograph brought to mind one of his favourite characters, Mr Pickwick. They not only looked alike, but Secombe liked to think he possessed some of the qualities he so much admired in Dickens's much loved character. Staying nearby in a house he had just bought was Wolf Mankowitz, the writer whose success owes so much to his ability for combining humour with sensitivity and compassion. He received an unexpected invitation to lunch, and over the meal Secombe put forward his rather vague idea for a musical extravaganza, based on the exploits of the Humpty-Dumpty man with gaiters, white breeches, bright waistcoat, steel-rimmed glasses and flat topped black hat.

Mankowitz, a broad, lion-headed man, was immediately won over and agreed to do an adaptation. When Secombe returned home he saw his agent, the Jimmy Grafton of those early Goon days, and he too was enthusiastic. The final hurdle was overcome when impressario Bernard Delfont, one of the brothers in the famous show business trio – Lew Grade and Leslie Grade are the others – agreed to stage it at the Saville Theatre.

The curtain went up in July 1963, and the show, with the book by Mankowitz and music and lyrics by Leslie Bricusse and Ornaldel, was greeted with rave notices by the critics. It had a long and successful run and went down well with American audiences, although there was near disaster in Detroit when Secombe's wig fell off as he was doing a cartwheel. Harry saved the moment by brandishing it like a scalp and shouting, 'Indians.' The audience roared with laughter at his nimble-wittedness and the show went on as if nothing had happened. Pickwick was, and still is, Secombe's favourite role.

From there Secombe went from triumph to triumph in films, television and the theatre. Like Sellers, his name in lights is an automatic guarantee of box office success.

His comic genius reached its peak in 1967 when he made a 37-minute film with Hattie Jacques, Eric Sykes and Graham Stark, during which the only word of dialogue was 'rhubarb, rhubarb, rhubarb'.

In 1971 the nation's top line entertainers turned out in force to pay homage to Harry's twenty-five years in show business at a Variety Club luncheon. And three years later the years were rolled back when Milligan, Sellers and Secombe got together and did an impromptu buskers' act in crowded Regent Street, for Harry's BBC television Christmas Show. Spike in a tatty, stained raincoat played the trumpet, and Sellers, in a tramp's overcoat, squeezed an accordion. Secombe, in a threadbare army greatcoat, played the fool and went round with the hat. They raised £4.75p, which they donated to charity.

The same year Secombe became accepted as a serious writer with the publication of his first novel, *Twice Brightly*, which was dedicated to Milligan, Sellers and Bentine. Although there was a lot of Secombe in the principal character, Gower, it was not autobiographical, neither was it a labour of love. For he had to be badgered by his family before he got around to completing it. But in the book he managed to express some of his personal views of life, expose the behind-stage aspect of entertainment, and the myth that it was all glamour, romance and easy money. He showed the disappointments and the heart-aches, and the incurable optimism an entertainer must have if he is not to disappear without trace. Equally important is his 'keep your feet on the ground' attitude to success when it finally does arrive.

He once summed it up this way: 'People like me live in fairy castles, pretending every night. If you're not careful, you can start believing your own publicity, and that's disastrous. It's killed many an entertainer.'

The only time a hint of boasting enters his talk is when he expresses views on today's young comedians. But his criticism is in no way carping; it is simply that he regrets there are so few outlets for them to learn the job properly. The music hall, that great college of comedy, is no more; even the Windmill is no longer there to provide a platform. Talking of the need to really master the art he said, 'I could go on to a TV programme like "New Faces" or "Opportunity Knocks" with a corny routine I once did, showing how different people shave, and be a hell of a lot more original than most of the youngsters you see on those shows.'

What he was saying was that show business, like any other profession, needs to be worked at. Success, unlike tinned coffee, isn't instant, so when it comes treat it with respect. 'You are working with laughter, a transient and intangible thing. It takes discipline and experience to keep control but until you do it you are not in business.' They are not carelessly tossed-away words. As the Vicar of Hanwell is quick to point out: 'There's another depth or facet to him – he is a thinking person. If you look at his library, you will see this. He has a tremendous interest, for instance, in archaeology and ancient civilizations. Sometimes I'm amazed at the erudite books he buys: I wouldn't buy them, I just pinch some from him to read from time to time. He's especially fascinated by the Greek civilizations. He's been to Knossos. He spent a holiday in Crete a few years ago. He loves to read and to talk, sometimes, of things of the mind. Harry can be very serious.'

Harry is fluent in half a dozen European languages but,

strangely, does not speak Welsh, his native tongue. He is well versed in word derivation, and no one needs a dictionary when he is around. And he reads so prolifically that the manager of a major London bookshop says: 'Harry practically pays our overheads.'

He also remains an incorrigible prankster as big brother has discovered, to his embarrassment: 'We were on the train one evening when the ticket inspector came in. I was wearing my dog collar – he always used to insist on me wearing my collar in case people swore in front of me. Very protective – and, anyway, I couldn't find my ticket. So Harry looked up at the ticket collector and said: "Watch him. He's not a real parson, you know. They call him Flash Fred." I said, "Don't you listen to him," but it was clear that the ticket collector didn't know whether or not to believe him. Harry kept on, and he was more than half convinced. I still couldn't find the ticket. I was searching frantically through every pocket, and Harry was telling the collector: "He's always doing this, getting free rides on the strength of his collar. Look, you can see he hasn't got a ticket." "Shut up," I kept telling him. "No, no," he said. "People have got to be told about you." Well, eventually I found the ticket, and the collector gave Harry a really old-fashioned going over, telling him he should be ashamed of himself. That's typical of Harry.'

On another occasion when he was appearing at the New Theatre, Cardiff, he went to watch Cardiff City in a vital home game. He caused near confusion by shouting 'Come on Clackworthy' whenever a certain player got hold of the ball. There was no such person in the team, but with Harry at full bellow his shouts could hardly be ignored. Irate fans kept turning to him saying, 'No, no, boy, that's not Clackworthy. We don't have one.'

Unperturbed, Harry replied, 'Oh, I'm sorry about that. He looks just like Clackworthy.' Then he was off again giving the name to one of the opposing players.

It was harmless, boyish, but immensely funny. It typified Harry's leg pulls, no one was ever hurt or held up to ridicule.

As the years creep up on him, he often talks about devoting

more time to writing, but it is unlikely he will ever retire completely. 'Retirement for me would be like living on a desert island. I would miss the life and my friends. Inside a month I would be out busking. People ask me where I get my energy. All I know is that I'm a happy person with a marvellous wife and kids, and I reflect that. I like to convey a sense of fun.'

Myra still remains 'my girl at the dance', and his most respected critic, and his family the most important thing in his life. There are four of them – Jenny, 26; David, 13; Andrew, 22; and Katy, 9. Myra was 43 when the youngest was born and a delighted Harry greeted the news with: 'Poor kid – she says at her age she should be about to become a grandmother, not a mother.' To millions of television viewers he quipped: 'Anyway, we're making sure it won't happen again ... she's moved into a house down the road.'

In a more serious strain he said, 'Our family planning has been marvellous. We have two families.' And his deep love for children can get him to confess that he wouldn't mind more of them.

There have been many better singers than Harry Secombe, and certainly more original and inventive comedians, but it is fair to say there has never been anyone in the laugh-making business who has commanded more respect or affection. It's a view expressed not only by the customers but by his fellow pros.

Harry is not blind to his own popularity but he accepts it with modesty and humility. 'There's no need for pats on the back,' he once said. 'I'm not working for posterity. I don't want a statue erected. If I'm remembered with a smile that's reward enough. "He made me laugh" is a good epitaph.'

That really sums him up. But there will be a deep sense of loss when that epitaph finally comes to be written.

Chapter Six

SELLERS – INVISIBLE MAN

Today Peter Sellers is one of a handful of truly great international stars. The word genius is used with pepperpot abandon whenever anyone talks or writes about him, and they have been doing that for a long long time now. He is without question one of the finest character actors the world has ever seen, and his name on a credit title is an automatic guarantee of a resounding success that doesn't need to rely on any box office blarney or publicists' puffs. He is a millionaire with the Midas touch but remains a man who is not motivated by cash rewards.

Yet throughout the years that Sellers has been a top line star he has remained an enigma in the eyes of the critics, friends close and distant, and that redoubtable band of showbiz writers and gossip columnists who have filled columns of newsprint with the rhetorical question, 'Who is the real Peter Sellers?' Rhetorical for the simple reason that they have all gone on to expound at great length that there is no such person. That he just doesn't exist in the flesh and blood. Sellers is an insecure introvert with no identity of his own; a colourless man who loses himself in a crowd of brilliant self-created characters. The myth has hung over his head like a sword of Damocles throughout most of his professional life, but Sellers is partly to blame, for he has aided and abetted it in countless interviews until the myth is accepted as reality.

Sellers doesn't like it clinging to him like a ghost from the past, for with the passing of the years he has matured and developed to such a degree that his professional life no longer takes over his private one. At home he can be Pete and cast off his latest character with the ease of a chameleon blending with the background.

But his fans and admirers still won't accept it.

Sellers to them is personified by the Jak cartoon which appeared in the *Evening Standard* the day after his marriage to the Swedish actress Britt Ekland, a girl with chocolate box beauty and stunning figure, at Guildford in 1964. It was satirical rather than funny for it depicted a puzzled-looking girl staring across the breakfast table at her faceless husband reading a paper with the headline SELLERS WEDS. Around the walls were portraits of some of his more memorable film characters. The caption below said:

So that's what you *really* look like!

Sellers was not amused. For him it had literally been love at first sight and he had married her after a whirlwind courtship that had lasted all of twenty-one days. No wonder he was piqued. He knew what he was marrying and didn't like the idea that she didn't.

Jak was not being malicious, he was simply exercising his inimitable gift for succinctly pinpointing in words and pictures what most people thought but couldn't express. He wasn't the first and he certainly won't be the last person to be intrigued by Sellers' incredible talent for making a character really come to life.

Not long before, the *Standard*'s rival the *Evening News*, had carried a line drawing of Sellers against a background of floodlights, booms and microphones which depicted a firm-jawed young man with wavy black hair and the male counterpart of a Mona Lisa smile. The drawing was more flattering than the couplet below:

So many faces, none of them his own;
So many voices, all of them on loan,
Until, confused, poor Peter Sellers asks,
'Who am I please, behind these endless masks?'

The lament has a touch of despair about it; a *cri de coeur* for a man who has lost his way in a labyrinth of his own making. Certainly that kind of Fleet Street psychoanalysis did him no harm; the public doesn't really want its idols to be open books. If you put someone on a pedestal you insist on them having a certain amount of mystique. Certainly there is no record of Sellers ever having objected to it; on the contrary, he perpetuated it in newspaper and magazine life stories.

Ironically, Peter Sellers *doesn't* officially exist. He was christened Richard Henry after his grandfather.

'From the very beginning – why I don't know – I was called Peter,' he recalls.

That in itself was unlikely to have had any real traumatic effect. Lots of people go through life with names that don't appear on their birth certificates. For a full understanding of the remarkable Sellers one has to delve deeply into his past and early upbringing and turn over the stones of memory. Only in that way does the jigsaw begin to take shape and a true picture begin to emerge. It wasn't a happy childhood. It was lonely, nomadic, while the purely physical aspects made it virtually impossible for him to have a stable boyhood. There were too many conflicting forces all pulling him in different directions.

At one stage the dream factories of Hollywood revelled in making lavish musicals about showbiz families' backstage life, with talented adolescents burning to follow in Ma and Pa's footsteps. When Judy Garland sang about being born in a trunk in the Princes Theatre it was just romantic escapist make-believe.

In Sellers' case it was only minutes away from being the truth. His mother Peg Sellers was appearing in a revue called 'Frivolities' at the King's Theatre in the naval town of Portsmouth. Although well advanced in her pregnancy, like the trouper she was, she had insisted on working until the last possible moment. On 8th September 1925, in the middle of her act, she experienced labour pains and knew her time was near. She told her husband Bill, who doubled as her chauffeur and pianist, to get her home to their flat in Southsea Terrace in record time. Bill Sellers almost pushed the accelerator through the floor boards of their ancient red Ford. But he made it and a bawling bouncing boy was brought into the world by a local G.P. in a room above a shop named Postcard Corner which eked out a precarious living selling picture views of HMS *Victory*, the dock-yards, and surrounding countryside. It was the beginning of a nightmare existence that has left scars on Peter Sellers which are still visible today.

Although his parents were happily married and doted on their son, it was a marriage that had inherent tug-of-war aspects. Peg was Jewish, Bill was a Protestant. As a result, Peter was to grow up without any true religion so that later in life he was to continually seek spiritual satisfaction in yoga, spiritualism, clairvoyancy and Christianity.

Peter's grandmother was a remarkably forceful woman with the unlikely name of Welcome. When she was widowed with a large family of young children in the sultry soot-grimed overcrowded streets of Hackney in London's squalid East End, she did not sit back and dwell on the harsh and brutal vicissitudes of life. She launched into a new life and formed Britain's first travelling review which was a bathing belle spectacular called 'Splash Me'. It centred round a vast glass-sided tank filled with water in which girls, scantily clad – for those days anyway – cavorted and dived. It was considered a trifle naughty and even daring: one aqua-beauty actually peeled and ate a banana under water to the strains of Handel's 'Water Music'.

The roving show flourished and Welcome, who became professionally known as Ma Ray, was a big crowd drawer at the music halls on which she descended in a roar of exhaust in the splendid crimson Ford. It was a car that was to be of crucial importance to Peter Sellers' existence for it was instrumental in bringing his parents together.

Ma had clawed her way from the near poverty of the East End to comparative luxury, and everyone admired her battling spirit and tenacity. They were inherited characteristics: there was a great family tradition of coming back fighting when you were down. Welcome was descended from Daniel Mendoza (1764–1836), a Portuguese-Jew from the near ghettos of Aldgate who became a bare knuckle pugilist and pounded his way to the heavyweight championship of England, and later became the companion of Royalty. Apart from the power of his brine-toughened hands there was a lot of the showman in him. He was a flamboyant peacock of a man who knew from experience the truth of the dictum that 'empty bellies make good fighters'. At the same time he was intelligent enough to recognize the fact that if you were clobbered enough you ended up punch-drunk, especially in an era when there were no gloves to cushion the impact of granite-hard knuckles. So Mendoza, the man the crowds dubbed 'The Light of Israel', turned fisticuffs into a fine art and wrote a treatise on *The Art of Boxing*.

The Prince Regent, later George IV, became his patron and Mendoza taught him the rudiments of the noble art. Daniel became a popular figure and songs were sung in his honour by an adoring public, but he nevertheless died a poor man.

To this day Peter Sellers is immensely proud of his forebear and is firmly convinced there is a great affinity between him and the long-dead fighter. Certainly his face and build bear a remarkable resemblance to early portraits of the swarthy good-looking fighter who did the full circle of rags to riches and back again.

There was never any serious doubt that his mother Peg would join Ma Ray in her theatrical ventures and during the First World War she was standing at the footlights belting out patriotic songs and the equivalent of today's Top Ten. In time she graduated to a tableau form of acting which was popular with audiences of the day.

With the war over and the Depression not yet even a spectre on the horizon, it was a time when the people really set out to enjoy themselves with uninhibited fervour.

Then in 1921 the course of Peg's life was dramatically altered by the chance encounter between her mother and a young man in a restaurant. His name was William Sellers and he was playing the kind of piano music that women like to half-listen to as they chat away over their cups of tea.

He was summoned to Ma's table, who told him, 'I need a piano player in my show. If you want the job it's yours.' There was one proviso. 'Can you drive?' He could, so the job was his.

Whether Ma Ray was looking solely for a driver-pianist or possible husband for her twenty-four-year-old daughter is purely speculative. But Peg Sellers seems to have taken an instant liking to the shy, quietly spoken Yorkshireman who came from dour but solid farming folk.

When he was quizzed about his past he explained that he had been the assistant organist at Bradford Cathedral and that he was a Protestant. It was a disappointment for Ma who would have preferred a Jewish lad, but it was obviously no obstacle to Peg.

The couple were married in Bloomsbury Register Office in 1923.

With such a background and heritage it was inevitable that Peter should be destined for a career in entertainment. Two weeks after his birth he was carried on to the stage by the show's comedian Dickie Henderson, father of the present star. It was a natural thing, for audiences then followed the lives and fortunes of their favourites with more genuine interest and affection than they do now.

Henderson held up the small bundle for inspection. 'Here's Peg Sellers' little son. Let's wish him well.'

The audience burst into a spontaneous rendering of 'For He's a Jolly Good Fellow' and the infant Sellers, dead on cue, bawled his head off. It was his first taste of laughter and applause.

But it was no life for a child. His parents were rootless, moving from town to town, theatre to theatre, digs to digs. All of which had a monotonous similarity, Sellers can conjure up those days with astonishing clarity, but the total recall is tinged with bitterness. 'I would stand in the wings watching matinee performances. I remember one act especially when my mother wore white tights and stood in front of a plain white screen. Behind the audience a magic lantern cast slides of different costumes on to the screen. The result was that my mother would appear as all kinds of women in history or mythology, from Britannia to Joan of Arc, and yet never really change.'

Seeing his mother as those heroines from the past and

hearing the rapturous reception that each change of character brought was the good part.

'My mother's act moved me in a way I still can't explain,' he said years later. 'She looked beautiful standing there like a white statue, the colour and the warmth and the applause and the feeling of being part of something that could give so much happiness to other people made me want to be up there with her taking a more positive part than just watching from the wings.'

The theatre, however, has another side the public doesn't see, and it was this that appalled Sellers. The constant moving, a new home each week, the lousy food and stench of half-cooked cabbage, musty sheets and mildew-damp rooms sickened him. They are smells which still clog his nostrils. They left an indelible impression. 'I have never liked the theatrical life and still don't,' he recalled. 'I didn't like the smell of warm greasepaint that would blow out to me in the wings, mixed with sweat and smoke and tiredness. I didn't like the theatrical digs and lodging houses, and I certainly had my share of them as a boy when touring with my parents and later when touring on my own. Every place had its own particular smell, depending on the nationality of the landlady.'

Peg Sellers didn't share his love-loathing attitude, for she was firmly convinced that her son would become a child prodigy. At three when he was still at the toddler stage she togged him out in a specially made Fred Astaire top-hat, white tie and tails outfit, complete with cane, and taught him to sing 'My Old Dutch', the tear-jerker hit of the old Cockney comedian Albert Chevalier.

Apart from being encouraged to play the part of an old trouper, there was a grave danger of the young Sellers growing old before his time, for his environment meant that he seldom mixed with lads of his own age and apart from missing the enjoyment obtained from normal kids' games his education was sadly lacking. He became self-sufficient in providing his own amusement. He learned to live within himself – not an ideal upbringing for a sensitive lad. He still

vividly recalls those digs and their effect on him. 'The bedrooms were all alike, with marble washstands and brass beds.
I'd look up at the ceiling and say to myself, "Oh, God, I do
wish we had a home." '

Perhaps those unspoken words communicated themselves
to Peg, for suddenly in 1933 when Peter was seven his mother
had a change of heart and decided he needed some permanency in his life and a home to call his own. She may
also have noticed that he was far too superstitious for so
young a child. When he was six his father walked out after
a domestic tiff and the small boy began to indulge in what
his mother called 'the imagines'. Perhaps she was afraid to
face up to the realities of what it really meant for Peter:
the number six assumed tremendous significance. He would
rise up and down on the toilet seat six times before finally
settling, and he had to pull the chain exactly the same number of times. So she moved to a house near Regent's Park
and her son was sent to St Mark's Kindergarten in Gloucester
Crescent, as a fee-paying pupil. Her stage days were over,
but Bill Sellers continued the rounds of the music halls playing the piano and ukulele in a turn that was never blazoned
in lights, nor the bringer of fame or fortune. But more important, his long spells away from home meant that Peter
was virtually brought up by his mother who was, in any
case, a much more forceful, dominant and possessive character than her husband. The result was that Peter's attitude and
outlook were firmly moulded into shape by Peg. She still
envisaged a theatrical career for him, although she was now
running a small antique shop in Highgate. With the move of
homes came a switch of school, and for some inexplicable
reason Peg sent the religiously neuter child to St Aloysius
College in Hornsey Lane, run by the brothers of Our Lady
of Mercy. They were relatively happy times, although he did
not leave any lasting impression on the school. He played
football in the playground with the brothers who rolled up
their habits and tucked them in their belts. (When they
wanted to retain possession they simply let their robes drop
so that the boys couldn't get at the ball.) He developed a

lifelong love of cricket and became a passable slow bowler. He also established himself as the class mimic with caricatures of the staff and was a bit of a schoolboy wit. A friend recalls that when the lads could only name six of the seven seas, Sellers piped up with 'The BBC'. He somewhat surprisingly excelled at religious instruction.

His form master was Brother Cornelius who still teaches at the infants school, but he has only a hazy recollection of Sellers. 'He was just average, not a memorable scholar, not a memorable athlete, not very outstanding at all.'

Later Sellers was to give Brother Cornelius celluloid immortality, for he based his characterization of the priest in 'Heavens Above' on his old tutor.

During school holidays Sellers would go 'totting' – with his mother, an uncle, and his father too if he was 'resting' between engagements – collecting old jewellery, antiques and bric-a-brac for sale in the shop. For one so young Sellers learned the doorstep patter with amazing speed and remarkable conviction.

Then what everyone knew was inevitable actually happened: Britain went to war against Hitler. Sandbag barriers altered the face of London and the nights were filled with the nerve-chilling wail of the sirens, and the rumble of falling buildings, as high-explosive bombs rained down from the bomb bays of the Luftwaffe's invisible but audible planes.

Night after night the Sellers crouched in their small air raid shelter listening to the seemingly non-stop destruction. Finally Peg Sellers called 'enough' and the family moved to Ilfracombe in Devon where an uncle managed the old seafront theatre The Victoria Pavilion. Peter was thirteen and that was the end of his formal education; something he has never ceased to regret, for despite an enormous amount of reading he still considers himself only half-educated.

Paradoxically, absence from the world of the theatre had re-kindled Sellers' enthusiasm; the smell of greasepaint was no longer anathema. He cheerfully took on the chores: billposting, shifting the seats when the theatre was turned into a temporary dance hall, polishing the ornate brass fittings, and clearing the ash trays of cigarette ends.

'My routine,' he recalled later, 'became set: to sweep the theatre out every morning, to sell tickets at the box office, and sometimes even manage the big spotlights that illuminated the stage.'

By the time he was fourteen, Peter was so proficient that he was allowed to light the stage on his own. For this he was paid the princely sum of ten shillings a week. But by now the young Sellers' ambition was to have the spotlights on him – he no longer wanted to bathe others in the limelight. Never the most self-confident of youngsters, his ego, however, got a tremendous fillip when with a young friend, Derek Altman, he won £5 singing a duet at a Sunday night talent competition. It was a shortlived partnership, for Derek wasn't bitten by the showbiz bug – he preferred something a little more reliable and less precarious. He became a barber.

Sellers carried on for a simple reason: 'There seemed nothing else that I could do.'

No one can predict how he would have fared as a solo singer for Joe Daniels and his Hotshots arrived at The Victoria Pavilion for a short engagement and the career course of Sellers was dramatically altered. Joe was a drummer of great skill and spectacular verve and Sellers, gazing from the wings with what amounted to near idolatry, was captivated. At night when the auditorium was deserted Peter would nip in and assume the mantle of Joe.

'In the empty theatre, lit only by a working light, I would take over his drums and let loose and enjoy myself. One day, just like in the movies, he found me at the drums and gave me some instruction. Finally, he let me sit-in on the drums with the band,' said Sellers.

Seeing that he was determined to make it a career, his parents bought him a set of drums and arranged for lessons in classical and free-style drumming, and before he was out of his teens he was playing with such established bands as Oscar Rabin and Henry Hall. For a time he became an ersatz gipsy in Waldini's Gipsy Band, wearing a flowing romany blouse with puffed sleeves and ruffed collar. It was money under false pretences. Waldini was a Welshman, and it is doubtful if any one of the troubadors had ever slept in a caravan. Certainly Sellers didn't know one end of a horse from the other.

But the non-stop travelling, the lousy lodgings, blacked out windows, the endless waits in chilly railway stations, and the same old stale sour smells rolled back the years, and the loathing he had experienced in early childhood returned. Sellers packed his drums, handed in his floral headscarf and headed for home. There his father invited him to tour with an ENSA party. Britain was going through one of the toughest patches of the war and any diversion from the grim realities of everyday living was welcomed; even the group of entertainers who travelled the roads in a decrepit van with a NAAFI piano lashed precariously to the back. It was an odd assortment of talent: an acrobat, a dancer, a girl who sang Deanna Durbin hits, Dad Sellers who played the piano, and Peter who played the drums, strummed a ukulele and did occasional impressions to pad out the show.

Sellers didn't know it, but his feet were now on the first rung of the ladder which was to bring him world-wide acclaim, vast wealth, a C.B.E., and a personal life that was either peaks of elation or troughs of despair. The tour also introduced him to sex. During an over night stop in Taunton the group was booked in to a lodging house owned by the local undertaker who did his embalming in the basement. The non-stop flow of people popping in and out with wreaths, and men carrying coffins, plus strange untraceable noises, unnerved Sellers who confided his fears to one of the girls. She shared them too and the outcome was inevitable. She left her bedroom door unlocked with an open invitation for him to share the comforting protection of her arms. Alas, like so many other young men's initiations into the mysteries of sex it was a total fiasco. Sellers tried to be Casanova without removing his dressing gown and pyjamas.

It may have been a humiliating experience, but Sellers tucked it away in the pigeon holes of his memory and many years later, as in the case of Brother Cornelius, he used it to professional advantage. When he played the bumbling, totally inefficient Inspector Clouseau in 'The Pink Panther' one of the film's most hilarious scenes was based on what had happened that night in Taunton. 'I don't think it was any funnier on the screen than it was in reality,' he recalls.

Sellers was eighteen, darkly good-looking with a physique he insisted (seriously) was an exact replica of his idol Daniel Mendoza, and the magic of the drumbeats had been supplanted by the clarion call to duty. The newspapers at the time were filled with the exploits of the Hurricane and Spitfire pilots of Fighter Command, while the newsreels repeatedly showed them performing victory rolls as they came in to land. Sellers decided to join 'The Few' and volunteered for flying duties. But his visions of valour were shot down by the RAF medicos: his eyesight was too poor for aircrew and he ended up as a wingless member of the RAF's lowest form of life – an A.C.H.G.D. – the initials hid the mundane job Aircraft-hand Ground Duties. His official number was 22230333.

Repetition has never appealed to Sellers, which is why he prefers films to stage appearances; the monotony of a long run has made him steer clear of the legitimate theatre. So when he found himself as an armourer's assistant monotonously loading machine gun bullets for other men to fire, he decided the time was ripe for a change of occupation. The heaven-sent opportunity came when forms were circulated inviting personnel to volunteer for jobs in entertainment. Sellers romped through an audition and was posted to Ralph Reader's Gang Show, which had enjoyed peacetime fame as a vehicle for talented Boy Scouts.

When Peter was posted to India, Peg Sellers' maternal instincts rose to the surface: she wanted the ground-trapped airman to come under the protective custody of *her* wing, but despite her endeavours to keep him in Britain, Sellers eventually joined the florid-faced Squadron Leader Ralph Reader who spoke with a mid-Atlantic accent although he was as British as steak and kidney pie.

In no time at all Aircraftsman Sellers was getting lots of

laughs by impersonating his boss. He also began to extend his range of characters, and it was at this stage that Sellers realized he had a remarkable gift for mimicry and characterization.

Later he tried to explain it. 'My personality is not as someone else said, a blank page on which something is to be written. It's just that early on in life I found that *sounds* fascinated me. I became a listener. My ears were a sound radar that picked up every noise blip. I didn't talk much, I listened and people thought I was shy.'

Sellers soon realized there was a ring of truth, at least as far as he was concerned, in the popular barrack room ballad 'Bless 'Em All' – there was no promotion this side of any ocean for him. Stuck as Aircraftsman 22230333 until the armistice, he decided that if he couldn't get the pay that rank brings with it he would at least enjoy the privileges. In the show's prop room there was a vast assortment of uniforms and Sellers would simply pick one that fitted him, then casually stroll into the Officers' Mess for a chat and a few gins and tonics. He was so confident of his own ability that he didn't fear exposure, while the risk of an officer becoming curious about the stranger was extremely unlikely. So many people were in transit that a fresh face aroused very little interest.

'I found it more agreeable,' he explained later, 'spending my time in the Officers' Mess than in the crowded other-ranks canteen. In good time I would withdraw from the bar and duly make my appearance with the Gang Show. In the early morning we would be off again to the next stop. No one knew or cared who the young officer in the bar was or where he had gone.'

Apart from the sheer pleasure of drinking ice-cold drinks in a comfort denied to the ranks, there was clearly something else that drove Sellers to take incredible risks. It was a kind of Russian roulette with outrageous impersonations as bullets: the suicide would come when someone unmasked him. From Flight Lieutenant – not a great risk for he was about the right age – he promoted himself to Squadron

Leader and even had the audacity to inspect the men's quarters. Despite the remonstrations of his pals who warned that he was too young and bound to be rumbled, Sellers parted his hair in the middle, stuck on a busy moustache and casually went from hut to hut asking if there were any complaints. He listened to many, promised they would be passed to the appropriate authority, then divested of his disguise he rejoined the men who told him about the visiting officer who really seemed to care about their welfare.

Even that interlude didn't satisfy him and he decided to try his hand at being a Sikh officer, for some squadrons had officers from the Royal Indian Air Force attached to them. But it was no hit and miss affair, Sellers spent hours perfecting the accent, copying their mannerisms and mentally recording recurring phrases such as 'Goodness, gracious me ... my fine fellow, how are you today?' Then he darkened his skin, put on a beard and turban and spent an enjoyable evening in the mess. (It is not related as a rib-tickling anecdote: the prank gives some insight into his character. Years later he pillaged through his memory bank and used it for the basis of the memorable performance he gave as an Indian doctor in 'The Millionairess'. Like a miser he never throws anything away that may come in useful at some future date.)

His *nunc dimitis* only came when he pulled off an outrageous hoax that even astonished him. One Christmas he dressed up as an Air-Commodore. 'Even to me this seemed to be pushing my luck a bit far, for I was barely nineteen,' he recalls. That was a classic understatement: you don't get to be Air-Commodore until you've put in a lot, lot, lot of time and a pension is just around the corner. Uniforms galore there may have been, but there were no make-up men available to add the necessary years to Sellers' appearance. All he had were a few tubes of greasepaint, a tin of talc to grey his temples, and nothing else, but a friend who was present has said that as he stood in front of the mirror Sellers seemed to suddenly age and assume the mannerisms, voice and tetchiness of a senior officer wearied by the burdens of a war that seemed endless.

Sellers ambled into the Officers' Mess where he was a little shattered to find a slightly sozzled Air Marshal. Regaining his composure Sellers immediately became engaged in a harrowing discussion, for the Air Marshal wanted to know what Tedder was up to. The Air Marshal, his arm wrapped conspiratorially around Sellers' shoulders, insisted, as he was newly arrived from Blighty, he should know all the answers. Sellers realized it was time to make a diplomatic withdrawal. With a mumbled explanation that he was attached to intelligence and thus his lips were sealed, he made a bee-line for the comparative safety of the Sergeants' Mess. There he delivered a stirring speech of Churchillian eloquence and mixed freely with the 'lads' and imbibed even more freely of their liquor. Although by now slightly tipsy himself, it was the voice of a sergeant slurred with emotion and booze that made him realize, like Cinderella, that time was running out – and fast. 'I would like to thank you very much, sir, and say 'ow much we appreciate your coming into our mess,' said the sergeant. 'All the compliments of the season to you, sir.' Whereupon he called upon his fellow sergeants for three cheers for the Air Commodore who unlike so many top ranking officers had taken the trouble to find out for himself how the other half lived.

Sellers paused at the door, inclined his head and muttered with genuine feeling, 'Good night to you all, and God bless you.' By then it was no longer an act, Sellers had become totally immersed in the character he had created in front of the dressing room mirror.

Not long afterwards the steeple bells were pealing joyfully. People danced in the streets, tossed themselves into the fountains in Trafalgar Square, drunk themselves into a state of euphoria, and looked forward to a new Utopia. The war was over. For Sellers it brought demob, a government handout suit, a little cash, a fortnight's emergency ration coupons, and the sudden realization that he had to start all over again. In his pocket reposed a letter that was unlikely to touch the heart of any agent. Attached to his release certificate was a personal note initialled by his Wing Commander: 'The above-named is strongly recommended for any work with entertainment.'

Sellers went home to his parents who were now living at 211B High Road, Finchley, N.2. He dusted his drums and began practising, but engagements were few and far between and he spent most of his time lounging around London's 'Tin Pan Alley' with other demobbed and unemployed musicians, most of whom seemed to be drummers with far more talent and experience. The occasional engagement turned up and Sellers found himself once more on the treadmill he so detested: trudging from town to town with the added burden of a cumbersome and shoulder-bending set of drums. But mainly it was queueing outside the doors of chill-blooded agents whose only words seemed to be: 'Nothing for you.' Their off-hand attitude so appalled him that when he eventually became a success he instructed his staff that all callers must be treated with respect and consideration. To make sure they heed his instructions, he frequently rings up with an assumed voice.

At one time he was so desperate for work that he grabbed at the offer to act as a barker for sideshows in a Norwich fair, but when he arrived at the City famed for having a church for every week of the year and a pub for every day, he was unable to find a bed for the night. The irrepressible Walter Mitty aspect of his personality took over and, remembering that along with Mendoza he could also claim Disraeli as an ancestor, he telephoned a hotel and announced, 'Lord Beaconsfield's secretary here. His Lordship requires a single room for one night only.' He turned up soon afterwards with his battered suitcase in his hand, to find everybody overwhelmingly impressed and fawning. Porters salaamed, chamber maids did little formal curtsies, the manager was all bows and scrapes. Sellers signed the visitors' book with a flourish that indicated it was well worth preserving for posterity, then headed for the fairground and the tonsil-torturing job of trying to attract customers.

When he returned for dinner the red carpet treatment was noticeably absent, the manager's voice had a chilling edge to it like an Arctic blizzard. 'Two gentlemen are waiting to see you, my lord.' The last two words were uttered with no hint of servility, just stark contempt. Across the lounge he saw two barn-shouldered men with highly polished shoes without toecaps, short cropped back and sides, and belted raincoats that were unmistakably military in their origin. They were plain-clothes officers from the RAF's Special Investigation Branch, who had been called in by the suspicious manager who thought the belted earl could be a deserter.

'Lord Beaconsfield?' queried one of the officers.

'Yes,' said Sellers, his confidence not yet totally eroded. 'What can I do for you?'

'Lord Beaconsfield?' posed the other officer. 'Wouldn't it be more correct to say 22230333 Aircraftsman Sellers?'

'You have a point there,' Sellers said meekly. 'It would.'

It was one of his less impressive performances, but it taught him a lesson he was never to forget. In his quest for perfection in the creation of a character the whole thing could be jeopardized by a slovenly approach to the minor details. A porter unpacking his suitcase had come across two squashed Woodbines in a packet. The noble lord had diminished somewhat in his estimation if that was all he could run to. A quick check of the visitors' book further disclosed that his estate was in the High Road, East Finchley.

Unmasked and humiliated, Lord Beaconsfield was allowed to stay the night – after all, he had paid for the room. In the morning he humped his own bag downstairs. The foyer was deserted and he slunk out like a dog with its tail between its legs. No one bothered to press charges.

The war was over and although the streets were illuminated once more, times remained dark, and there seemed no light at the end of the tunnel of despondency the country was travelling through. A mood of gloomy despair seemed to have settled like a pea-soup fog. Sellers, never the most buoyant of individuals, suffered agonies. Too hard up to buy a car, he found that lugging his drums from town to town was an intolerable burden, so he switched to a more manageable instrument – the ukulele. He took lessons from his father who could claim he had taught the great George Formby, the toothy songster-comedian who did anything with an ukulele except make it talk. For a brief spell Bill Sellers became close to his son. For the first and last time he edged Peg on to the sidelines. But Peter was too talented and too quick a learner for the close companionship to last, and soon Peg was back in her self-appointed role as pilot of his fate and charter of his career. It was a good thing in many ways, for although Peter suffered periods of immense gloom and depression, Peg unswervingly retained her unshakeable faith that one day in the not-too-far-distant future she would see his name in lights.

Sellers reached his nadir in Peterborough where a music hall audience gave him the bird and let him know with Midlands bluntness exactly what they thought of his act. It happens at some time or another to every act, but Sellers felt it more deeply than most.

'To stand on a stage and be the centre of such hostility is a frightening experience. I was literally shaking when I came off,' he was to recall years later when he was a star and could fill any theatre. But it was apparent that the memory of that awful moment had not been expunged. 'During the interval between houses the manager came to the dressing room I shared with six others, and handed me a cheque for £12. "You're no good here, Sellers boy. Here's your money. There's no need for you to appear again." I sat there miserably, determined not to give up, but not knowing what to do,' he said.

Then came the kindly intervention of singer Dorothy Squires who was topping the bill with a belt-it-out style of ballad singing which would one day make her one of the few artists who could pack the Palladium. She urged the manager to let him stay till the end of the week. A bemused manager, anxious not to offend his leading lady, acquiesced but said he thought she had a strange sense of humour. 'He must be the worst comic in the business,' he said.

Although Sellers saw the week out he had serious misgivings about a future as an entertainer; he feared he was living on borrowed time. Next time there might not be a fairy godmother in the wings in the shape of another Miss Squires. Certainly the news that he had died the death in Peterborough was not long in reaching that world of agents, and the men who book their properties, and where every other word is a superlative and the tungsten-tempered hearts are worn on sleeves.

Sellers seriously considered throwing it in and concentrating on life as a professional photographer. It was not the despairing act of a drowning man; he was a remarkably good photographer who had tackled the art of picture taking with the same dedication he devoted to his impersonations. Today he could have a very lucrative existence taking commissioned pictures for glossy magazines and periodicals, and he has been privileged to take pictures of the Royal family.

It was only the undiminished faith of Peg which stopped him taking the plunge. That, plus a little bit of a nudge from Lady Luck without which no person, no matter how brilliant, can ever make the top. One day during one of his despondent treks through theatreland he bumped into an agent who suggested he try his comedy routine out on that veteran impressario Vivian Van Damn, who ran the Windmill Theatre, where naked girls posed before an audience of grubby-raincoated men who had to be warned by a lantern slide that binoculars were not allowed. But surprisingly it was a nursery for talented comics and the plaque of honour outside bore the names of many famous stars who had been launched there. Many other names were unrecorded, for the Windmill was a battleground where many an aspiring artist had met his Waterloo. You had to be really good to maintain the interest of a purely male audience.

Sellers was auditioned in Mr Van Damn's office and promptly offered a contract of £25 a week. 'I like your act,' he said with businesslike brevity.

After six weeks Sellers was again out of work. Mr Van Damn had not altered his opinion of the young ex-serviceman's talents, it was simply that no one stayed too long at the Windmill. He underlined his faith in his own judgement by instructing a sign writer to add Sellers' name to the plaque which stated: Stars of Today Who Started Their Careers In This Theatre. It was an unexpected accolade for the shrewd Mr Van Damn usually waited to see that his proteges had made it before adding their names to the roll of honour.

Sellers' name appeared below that of a man called Harry Secombe. Soon they would meet and a long and lasting friendship would be fused. More important, career-wise they were to be instrumental in forging a new and previously undreamed-of brand of zany comedy.

In the meantime, Sellers was once more pavement-bashing and doing the rounds in search of work. There was no lack of faith in his own ability, the problem was to get someone to listen. Sellers hit upon his own novel way of achieving this. From his parents' home in Finchley he telephoned Roy Speer, a top BBC producer; a nasal-voiced switchboard operator asked who was calling. Sellers, knowing that if he gave his own name the call would never be put through, said, 'This is Kenneth Horne here,' in the rich plummy tones of the comic whose voice was a welcome sound in millions of homes. Sellers was promptly put through to the producer's secretary.

This is how Sellers himself describes the hoax call.

'Good morning,' I said. 'I wonder if I could have a word with Roy? Kenneth Horne, here.'

'Certainly, Mr Horne.'

There was a click and a voice answered, 'Hullo, Ken, what can we do for you?'

'I've got Dickie Murdoch here with me. We saw a fellow the other night who we think might be good for your show. A most amusing impersonator – didn't you agree, Dickie?'

'Oh, absolutely. First rate,' I said, agreeing with myself in Murdoch's voice.

'What's his name?' asked Speer.

'Peter Sellers.'

Sellers swears he could almost hear the sound of Roy

Speer writing down the name. The time had come for the make-or-break revelation.

'I am Peter Sellers,' confessed the caller. 'Neither Mr Horne nor Mr Murdoch know anything about this, but at least I've proved I can do impersonations. It seemed the best way of getting an audition.'

There was an uneasy silence, then Speer burst out laughing. 'You're a cheeky young beggar. You certainly took me in. Come round and we'll see if we can fix something up.'

If it proved one thing to Peter, it also proved something else to the man he was shortly to meet, Spike Milligan. Milligan who has a penchant for analysing other people's actions thought the whole thing was very revealing. 'He has never been able to sell himself, you see. To make money out of himself as himself he wouldn't get to first base. He is just a nice, very quiet, and very complex simpleton. He is the most complex simpleton in the entire world,' he told Peter Evans, the author of a best selling biography of Sellers. Evans, who has known Sellers for a great many years, shares Spike's views, for he gave his book the enigmatic title *The Mask Behind the Mask*. While it is true that there are as many sides to Sellers' character as a cut diamond, the explanation of his call to Speer could be that he simply wanted to impress upon him his ability as a mimic. Whatever the motive, it certainly put Sellers on the road to stardom.

Speer gave him a spot in the radio programme called 'Show Time' in which he did a number of impersonations which naturally enough included Horne and Murdoch. Leslie Ayre, the radio critic of the London *Evening News*, enthused about the new discovery. Under a three column headline 'This Mimic is "Tops"' he wrote on Saturday, 10th July, 1948: 'O. Henry once spoke of an actor who did "impersonations of well known impersonators". Certainly many mimics give far too little study to their origin. Peter Cavanagh is an exception. And now, in Peter Sellers, radio brings us another really conscientious artist and a genuine rival to "Cav".'

It was a generous tribute, for Cavanagh was the undisputed

monarch of mimicry. After giving a few biographical details, Ayre went on to say 'His first broadcast in "Show Time" brought a scurry of agents; he's already fixed up a long series of Sunday concerts all over the country; and Roy Speer immediately booked him for the first available return date in "Show Time" – August 19.'

Sellers bought an eighteen-inch by ten-inch linen-covered green ledger and stuck in his first rave review. His proud mother had it framed and hung it on the wall. On the front page of the book he printed PETER SELLERS in two-inch-high block letters. Surrounding the name was a galaxy of small stars. (Today there are a dozen or more cuttings books most of them with red linen covers, and as his fame grew the name PETER SELLERS began to be embossed in gold letters.) Sellers' enterprising agent had the cutting reproduced alongside a photograph of a smiling, wavy-haired Sellers and inserted it in the trade magazines under the heading 'Radio's New Sensation – Peter Sellers – Speaking for the Stars'. It paid dividends for in *Show World* on August 25 the following item appeared. 'As a result of his second successful broadcast last Thursday in "Show Time", Peter Sellers has received several offers and negotiations are pending for a spot in one of the Radio series in the autumn. In the meantime the new quick-fire impressions will be heard in "Henry Hall's Guest Night" on Saturday, September 4th, and he makes his first appearance in "Variety Band Box" on Sunday, September 19th.'

Sellers had arrived, for both shows had a listening audience of millions. Within the short space of a year he had made more than one hundred broadcasts including 'half an hour of satirical wit and modern burlesque' on the highly prestigious Third Programme. He displayed his incredible virtuosity by condensing 'Ten Years of ITMA', the famous Tommy Handley show, into four minutes, during which he imitated no fewer than fourteen voices. There seemed no limit to the range of the indiarubber voice; he produced the rousing stentorian tones of Winston Churchill for the film 'The Man Who Never Was', and when for legal reasons John Huston the

American film maker wanted a few extra lines of dialogue for 'Beat The Devil', he obligingly impersonated the not-available Humphrey Bogart; he also produced the voices for the chimps in the world famous tea advertisement. In fact, he could have made a more-than-comfortable living just providing voices for commercials and sound-only film parts. He had a regular spot on Ted Ray's show 'Ray's a Laugh', and some of his own creations like Crystal Jollybottom became household names while his catch phrases were being repeated in offices, factory canteens and pubs. In addition he was appearing in theatres up and down the country, and in October 1949 he was second on the bill to Gracie Fields at the London Palladium. He had gone a long way in a very short time.

However, he was far from satisfied; apart from his inborn loathing of the variety theatre circuits he was already looking ahead to something more original than merely taking off other people. More and more he was determined to become a character *actor*, and he realized that the ideal vehicle for his unique talents was the cinema. The theatre was virtually ruled out because of its essentially repetitive nature, and although he frankly admits the Goon years were among his happiest he would never have been content to have remained a disembodied array of voices even if the series did achieve cult proportions. Ironically although he has achieved cinematic immortality he has never been able to shake off the tag ex-Goon. Not that he ever wants to: the Goons provided an idyllic period in a life that has brought wealth and acclaim but no surfeit of happiness or contentment.

As *Daily Express* drama critic, songwriter and author Herbert Kretzmer, a close and longstanding friend of Sellers, wrote in 1960: 'Here is a man who has everything. He is the most successful actor since Olivier and Guiness. He enjoys a riotous acclaim clear across the world. He has more money than he can spend in his lifetime – and the endless promise of more ... Yet Peter Sellers is one of the saddest, most self-tortured men I have ever known. Here is a man almost devoid of any capacity to sit back and enjoy the riches his genius has produced. There is certainly no more complex personality in the whole spectrum of British show business. On the surface Peter Sellers is a man riding the giddiest tidal wave of success. His films span the globe, shimmering with triumph. His mere presence in a movie cast is practically a guarantee that the film will become a box office miracle. But as the idolatrous clamour for Sellers rises in volume, so the man at the storm centre increasingly retreats within himself, consciously withdrawing from the world that seeks to do him honour.'

It wasn't just a writer producing an extremely professional piece of profile writing; it was a close friend analysing a man he admires, respects and likes.

When Mr Kretzmer was asked if he would give permission for his views to be quoted he readily agreed, and when asked if his views had changed or modified in any way he said they hadn't: he would still write today what he wrote so many years ago. His views are worth noting for he not only knows Sellers socially but has also written hit songs for him. He endorses his own views by recalling a conversation he had with Peter.

'Sellers has no delusions about himself — "I have no confidence in myself. I have no push. I am terribly aware of my shyness and reserve ... People, you see, are wrong about me. They're all wrong. They see me on television, they hear my records. They think I'm a terribly funny and witty fellow, so they ask me to bazaars and cocktail parties and dinner parties, and expect me to be funny all the time. I can't do it. I just can't. Don't underestimate the effect of this, day after day, on the nerves and my patience; I dry up. I am afraid to open my mouth. I really am a negative person." '

Kretzmer then gave what he considers is the real answer to Sellers' bewildering personality. 'I know what Peter Sellers is looking for. And so does he. And, what is more important, he knows he will never find it. He is a man continually, restlessly in search of absolute perfection. This is the only real prize towards which he strives with such anguish and dedication.'

When Kretzmer wrote that, Sellers was married to his

first wife Anne and had two lovely children, Michael and Sarah, a magnificent country mansion at Chipperfield and the world at his feet. But the marriage ended in bitterness and disillusion after eleven years.

No one likes raking over the ashes of burnt-out loves, but it is essential if one is to ever get a full, clear picture of Sellers as a man and as an artist who can make millions roar with laughter whether as an outrageously exaggerated Goon character, or a brilliantly etched portrait of someone like Kite the shop steward in 'I'm All Right Jack'.

Sellers was twenty-three when he first met Anne Hayes, a nineteen-year-old student from the Royal Academy of Dramatic Art who was living with her family in Hendon. She was an attractive girl with shortish, wavy blonde hair and a warm disarming smile, and her tuition at RADA had removed all signs of her down-under accent. It was – to use that overworked cliché – 'love at first sight', but it was far from being a whirlwind courtship. In the first place Peter's mother was opposed to it; she argued that Anne was not of the Jewish faith, but as Sellers wasn't either, and Peg had herself married a Protestant and later sent Peter to a Catholic college the objection lacked conviction. The more likely reason was that she did not want another woman usurping her position. That Peg Sellers exercised a far too important influence on her son is without question. Spike Milligan who lived in the Sellers' household for some time when he had nowhere else to go observed critically, if a little uncharitably, that Peg waited on him hand and foot. Whenever Peter wanted anything she would jump up and attend to his needs. And when Sellers was on tour he seldom failed to telephone her, sometimes spending an hour on the phone. 'It is unhealthy for a grown man to be so needful of his mother,' Spike said.

One doesn't have to agree with Milligan, and a lot of Sellers' friends don't, but they all agree that he was devoted to his mother and genuinely anxious not to hurt her. That probably explains why he and Anne waited until 26th April, 1950 to announce their engagement. Not that it made headline news. If Sellers' own cuttings book is a reliable guide only one newspaper, the now defunct *Star*, mentioned it. Underneath an arm-in-arm picture of the smiling couple it captioned:

Her Man's A Scream. Twenty-year-old Melbourne actress Anne Hayes who lives now in Hendon with her mother has become engaged to radio comedian Peter Sellers whose 'You Old Saucebox' is one of the screams of 'Ray's a Laugh'.

In a later edition it was reduced to a single-column picture of Anne.

Success came quickly. Apart from the success of The Goons, Sellers was steaming ahead in his film career. He played in 'The Lady Killers' with Sir Alec Guiness, 'The Naked Truth', and 'The Mouse that Roared'. Guiness had for long been Sellers' idol and it was after a party to celebrate the actor's knighthood that Sellers appeared on the stage at the Aldwych Theatre where he was playing in 'Brouhaha' and announced to an astonished audience, 'I'm sloshed.' While he could remember his lines he had a little trouble getting his tongue round them, so he asked the audience if they wanted him to continue. 'Let's have a show of hands,' he said. The forest of arms that shot up made it clear that they wanted him to carry on. Sellers isn't the first and won't be the last actor to step on the stage a little the worse for wear, and the story wouldn't be worth mentioning if it didn't shed some light on his make-up. Naturally some of the papers picked up the confession and turned it into first rate copy. Thinking of the damage it could do to his career his friends and business associates advised him to say it was all a publicity stunt, but he refused. His integrity, such an essential ingredient to his work, wouldn't allow him to take the easy way out.

As Sellers is the first to recognize, the turning point in his career came at a charity cricket match at Totteridge, Herts., where he turned out for a side captained by John Boulting, one half of the famous Boulting Brothers film-making team. After the match John casually mentioned that he had the ideal part for Sellers in a film called 'I'm All Right Jack' which was a send-up of factory life. He wanted him to play the role of Fred Kite, a pompous, self-opinionated shop steward who was a tyrant on the factory floor and a hen-pecked little man with no authority at home. At first Sellers was unconvinced that it was a part for him, but eventually he was filibustered into accepting it. It was one of the cinema's most memorable performances for as Boulting said, 'He wasn't Sellers at all. He was a man called Kite.'

Sellers, with his obsession for perfection, totally immersed himself in the role to such an extent that he lost his own identity. He became remote, aloof and detached and withdrew more and more into himself. He studied newsreel films of trade unionists, listened to their speeches, copied their mannerisms. He recalled recently, 'There was a spate of strikes at the time so it wasn't very difficult getting material. I really did live the part. I had my hair cut Gestapo short and rarely went out.'

A framed 'wedding day' picture which occupies a place of honour in Sellers' home shows him with his film wife Irene Handl. The Hitler moustache, ill-fitting suit, the ostentatious breast pocket handkerchief, the smug look, are all so perfect that one finds it hard to accept that it is only a role he is playing. It wouldn't be out of place on the mantelpiece of a flesh-and-blood shop steward.

His performance got rave reviews and it was so realistic that one or two trade union officials took umbrage, while a special film showing was laid on for Members of Parliament at Westminster because it was considered of social significance. But Sellers was to pay an extremely high price in terms of personal happiness for total absorption in his roles. And he is the first to admit it. 'When I assume a character it takes over my personality completely. I find myself slipping into an almost trancelike state. The character takes me over. He exists in my body. I don't have to ask myself how he would react to this or that. I know the character acts for me ... During the production of a movie I lunch alone in my dressing room to keep the trance intact. I try not to talk to anyone, become interested in anything that would not interest the character.'

Such dedication is marvellous for the people who will sit in the cinema and see the final result, but it spelt domestic suicide for Sellers. When he went home after a hard day's filming he was unable to shed the character. 'Anne never knew who would be coming home to her. It must have been difficult for her to live with me during some of my films,' he said candidly.

When he played the part of the Indian doctor opposite Sophia Loren in the film version of Bernard Shaw's 'The Millionairess', the fictional character completely took over again. 'Once during the film,' he wrote in the *Sunday People*, 'an Indian came up to me in the street and said quite seriously that I was the new Messiah, that I should lead India into new paths. I even began to feel I could heal people. It was frightening.'

When his mother went to lunch with him on the set, she found herself dining with an Indian doctor.

Few marriages could withstand such pressures, and Anne's was no exception. The last straw must have come when with the same compulsive honesty that he had shown at the Aldwych he confessed to her that he had fallen in love with his leading lady. It would not be too far-fetched to suggest that the truth was more likely that the character he had become had fallen in love. The on-screen romance *had* to become off-stage reality.

In a genuine attempt to save the dying marriage, Sellers sold his half-Tudor Queen Anne mansion at Chipperfield, with its huge gardens, stables, swimming pool and retinue of servants, and moved into a penthouse suite overlooking Hampstead Heath. He employed a South African architect, Ted Levy, to do the designing and interior decor which meant he was a constant companion of Anne's. 'By then,' said Sellers, 'I had come to realize how much I needed and loved Anne.'

But it was too late – she had fallen in love with Levy and one day she announced she was leaving and that they would marry as soon as the divorce came through.

It was a bitter blow for Sellers who lost himself in work and got the reputation of a womanizer; something which he makes no attempt to deny. 'Many of my dates ended up in bed, because that's how they were destined to end.' There is a touch of sadness in the confession, for Sellers was seeking happiness which had always seemed to elude him. Even when his marriage was set and stable he had told Herbert Kretzmer, 'Damnit, if I'm ever going to be happy surely the time is now! I've got everything, everything. Two lovely kids. And Anne. God, I don't want another wife. I don't want other children except my own. Well, what's wrong? Why can't I be happy now? What am I looking for?'

There is one facet of Sellers' multi-sided make-up that many people find hard to stomach, let alone understand, and that is his surprising streak of ruthlessness. The man who can show astonishing generosity towards his friends has also been known to toss them to the wolves, if he felt they did not measure up to *his* expectations. It's a characteristic that is not uncommon in the rat-race of big business – inefficiency can't expect to be cushioned by the old pals act – but sometimes Sellers callously jettisoned a friend after exercising his vast influence to ensure that they got a particular job on a film with him. His own judgement, it seems, is never at fault; it's always the other person who is out of step. His sudden lack of confidence in others is never seen as a lack of self-confidence. Even more irrational is his genuine surprise that people have been wounded by his actions.

Dennis Main Wilson saw nothing inconsistent in Sellers insisting on working at getting someone a job, then getting rid of them. 'It's perfectly understandable, if not forgivable,' he said. The explanation was, that one side of Sellers wanted to help a friend or colleague, while the perfectionist was not prepared to let anything stand in the way of a successful film. So by giving a friend a job and then getting rid of him both sides of his tug-of-war nature was satisfied. 'He's a difficult sod to work with, but given all that talent who wouldn't be?'

There is no shrewder observer of the entertainment scene

than Main Wilson, but his explanation is an oversimplification, as the story related by author Peter Evans reveals.

Peter Evans, author of *The Mask Behind the Mask*, spoke recently of what it was like being at the receiving end of that professional toughness which gives scant regard to other people's feelings.

When he first began researching for the book, with Sellers' full co-operation, he was working for the *Daily Express* where he was headlined as 'Britain's greatest show business writer'.

'Sellers was very enthusiastic to start with and he spent a lot of time talking into a tape recorder. He would even phone me at midnight to talk about the book. I quit the *Daily Express* on the strength of doing the book, and before really immersing myself in it I went on holiday to Malta with my wife and children. One morning my secretary telephoned me in a panic to tell me that Sellers had written calling off the arrangement. It was quite a shock as I didn't have a job. His letter dated 12th September, 1966 said, "Dear Peter, I have given a great deal of thought to our proposed project on my life story, including dying and everything, and I have a very strong feeling that this is not the time to do it, although I think your idea generally is the best of all. In the words of Fred Kite, 'I have withdrawn, mediated, consulted and communed, and my decision has been democratically arrived at'." '

Said Evans, 'He expressed the view that the book was eight to ten years too soon, and his letter went on to say, "Of course it may be that nobody will be interested in me by then, but the reverse also applies and I know I am just coming into my most productive period right now. I trust you will understand my feelings, Peter, and not be too despondent." To say I was despondent was putting it mildly. I'd chucked my job and the book had been commissioned. Furthermore, I just couldn't see how the decision had been democratically arrived at. I hadn't even been consulted.'

Evans promptly caught a plane to Rome where Sellers was staying, and succeeded in getting him to change his mind; but soon afterwards he changed it again: no book.

Evans had no option but to go ahead with an unauthorized life which turned out to be a best-seller on both sides of the Atlantic. Sellers stubbornly refused to read it.

Said Evans, 'Ironically, as it turned out, the next few years were not his best, he went into a decline. They were the somewhat barren years. Only now is he beginning to put it all together again.'

Evans could be excused for feeling bitter, but he isn't and it illustrates yet again the remarkable hold that Sellers can retain over his friends, even when he's landed one below the belt.

'Despite the way he behaves,' said Evans, 'I have an intense respect for him. He buggers you around as a person, but fundamentally he is a very nice guy – if you don't get too close to him. He's fine as a friend if he doesn't need you and you don't need him. I'd hate to be involved with him professionally on a book or screenplay. As an artist he is so self-protective that he will do anything to maintain his independence. No one else matters if he thinks his artistic integrity or his opinion is at stake.'

A blunt and forthright appraisal. Yet Evans and Sellers remain good friends; they can still meet for a meal or a drink and not even mention *The Mask Behind the Mask*.

Peter Evans, like his fellow writer Kretzmer, remains captivated by Sellers, 'warts and all'.

Sellers dismisses, 'I have a reputation for being a shit' by saying that such criticisms are motivated by jealousy.

Some of it may be, although surely Evans cannot fall into that category. The original book was motivated by his admiration for Sellers.

For a large proportion of his adult life Sellers has been deeply interested in clairvoyancy and he regularly consulted the famous Maurice Woodruff who had impressed even the most cynical people with the accuracy of his predictions. He told Sellers a lot about himself which the actor knew could not have been discovered by simply reading up on his past. He forecast, for instance, that he would play the role of an

Indian doctor and the part would involve water. In 'The Millionairess' the first scene shows Sellers rowing a boat. Woodruff had also predicted the sex and birth dates of his children and told him that he would star in a film with a producer whose name began with Z. 'The Naked Truth' was produced by Mario Zampi. Woodruff also told him he would play in 'I'm All Right Jack' which jetted him to stardom. Therefore one can imagine the explosive impact of the sensitive Sellers when Woodruff told him he would marry a girl with the initials BE.

The prediction came true when Sellers was staying in the over-ornate Oliver Messel suite in London's Dorchester Hotel. One day he happened to be in the foyer when he saw an extremely beautiful young girl buying magazines from the bookstall. He recognized her as the Swedish actress Britt Ekland who was here to film in 'The Guns of Batasi'. Sellers was still deeply wounded by the break-up of his marriage and very vulnerable, and the girl made an immediate impression on him. One can't help speculating that the words of Maurice Woodruff also came to mind. The outcome was that Sellers sent his valet Bert Mortimer to her room with an invitation to join him for a drink; at the same time Bert added that Mr Sellers would like to take some portrait photographs of her. Ten days later he proposed, and twenty-one days after their initial meeting they were married at Guildford Register Office. It was a picture book wedding. Thousands turned up to watch, the snow fell, and the bride looked stunning in a mink coat and dress of 'wild white silk'. Peter's mother, the diminutive Peg, was there in scarlet, Britt's parents had flown over from Sweden. Peter's children Michael and Sarah seemed to have taken to their new 'Mum'.

Sellers posed dutifully on the threshhold of his nearby country cottage with Britt in his arms; they cut the cake; she showed her wedding ring and talked about the new Lotus car he had bought her along with the mink. Spike Milligan sent off a Goon-style telegram: 'You rotten swine, Bluebottle. You promised to marry me. Send me back the ring – Eccles.'

Soon afterwards Sellers went to Hollywood to film, and

Britt followed him, walking out of her film and involving him in a massive £714,280 breath of contract action. Sellers had rented a typical Hollywood-star-style home overlooking fashionable Sunset Boulevard. The floors were cool marble to compensate for the Californian heat, there were exotic plants and shaded patios, and Michael and Sarah, on Easter holidays from school, were there to share his new found happiness.

On 6th April, 1964, just seventeen days after the wedding, Sellers had a 'moderate coronary'. It was something he had feared, without any real justification, for some time. His father had died of a heart attack and Sellers frequently thought he was suffering one. Milligan said somewhat unsympathetically, 'He had about forty heart attacks before the real thing turned up.'

One evening Sellers said he was feeling a trifle tired and jaded and wanted to retire to his room to study the script for the film 'Kiss Me Stupid'. On the way to his room he paused, turned and asked Britt to call Dr Rexford Kennamer, one of America's foremost heart physicians. What had at first seemed just an acute attack of indigestion had now turned his chest into a blazing cauldron. Sellers, who had read a lot about coronaries, sensed the worst. Hadn't Woodruff warned him to expect 'a spot of bother'? He was taken to the fashionable Cedars of Lebanon Hospital in Los Angeles and installed in a private suite and given sedatives. Britt was allowed to move a camp bed into his room. But no one was unduly worried. Sellers, a judo expert, always kept himself reasonably fit. Furthermore he was only thirty-eight and mild attacks at that age are quickly overcome. When Peter fell asleep Britt returned home. A few hours later she was hastily summoned back to the hospital: her husband was in the intensive care unit after he had been found unconscious with no blood pressure or pulse. Prompt resuscitation had brought back some faint glimmer of life and now it was just a question of waiting and hoping. When Britt arrived at the third floor unit a nurse informed her that Sellers had suffered two massive coronaries. He wasn't given much hope.

Sellers recalled later, 'There were cords, cables, wires and tubes all over me, attached to a multitude of electronic devices which fed me, measured my pulse and heartbeat and kept me alive.'

Heavily under sedation he did not fully appreciate what was going on. 'It was like a mad Goon sketch with Bluebottle crying: "You've deaded him."'

Later he was to learn that his heart had stopped eight times. The first time his circulation stopped for a minute and a half. Once a doctor restarted his heart with a savage blow on the chest. The other times it was started by an electrical charge. Sellers literally died for a short period.

'But I never knew that I was living in the shadow of death,' he was to say much later. 'It seemed to me that I was just constantly dozing off.'

Sellers who had so often felt himself unloved and unwanted was amazed at the genuine grief his illness aroused. People did not weep for a great actor but Sellers the man.

Although Sellers had studied many religions and embraced none, he was deeply moved when his friend Father John Hester, a Church of England priest who works in Soho, flew to his bedside to anoint him and offer up prayers.

In newspaper offices the obituaries were being polished and honed and prominent figures in the entertainment world were being canvassed for their tributes.

Donald Zec, the *Daily Mirror* writer, said, 'Something had to give. No film star, even with a heart made of steel, could keep up Sellers' ferocious pace of picture-making. And today he lies in a Hollywood Hospital after a heart attack.

'Urgently, furiously, almost pathologically he has plunged from one film into another.'

In 1960 alone he made four major films and was voted Actor of the Year. His 11-minute short 'The Running Jumping Standing Still Film' which he made with Milligan was nominated for an Oscar. And in the incredibly short period following he made 'Doctor Strangelove – or How I learned to stop Worrying and Love the Bomb', 'Lolita', 'Only Two

Can Play', 'Waltz of The Torreadors', and 'The Pink Panther'. It was a phenomenal achievement for even his high output standards.

Newspaper switchboards were flooded with calls from people who wanted the latest news. The headlines proclaimed 'Chance if he gets past the Next Hours', and 'The 48 Critical Hours'.

The obits were premature. Sellers rallied and made a complete recovery, and six months later he was back at work as hard as ever. It was difficult to imagine what strange compulsion made Sellers consult Maurice Woodruff almost exactly four years after his 'death' and marriage, but he did and the man who had warned him in advance of the heart attack now told him his marriage was soon to end. Two months later Sellers announced in Rome that he and Britt were to get a divorce.

She returned home to Stockholm saying, 'I don't like the way he allows his life to be governed by soothsayers.' But she added, 'The strange thing is I know in my heart that if I had the choice I would do it again. He is a genius. Impossible, moody, temperamental, jealous, all those things, but life with him was extraordinary, stimulating, memorable.'

Sellers has soared to even higher pinnacles as an actor since then, but still the bluebird of happiness has eluded him. He fell in love with Liza Minelli but it was a short-lived romance. In 1970 he married Miranda Quarry, the stepdaughter of Lord Mancroft, but that ended very quickly on the grounds that it had irretrievably broken down.

Sellers said ruefully, 'I don't think marriage is my game. I mean, I'm unlucky at it, aren't I?' But he would like to marry again providing he could find the right woman. Is there such a thing as the perfect woman for him? At times of depression he looks nostalgically at the past and thinks of what might have been.

Milligan once remarked somewhat prophetically, 'The truth is he knows that yesterday he was happier than he can ever be tomorrow.'

In July 1975, Peter spoke with Clive Hirschorn of the

Sunday Express of 'those good, uncomplicated days with Spike Milligan and Harry Secombe when we were doing The Goons. That was the happiest, most informative time of my life. And, in a sense, the most vital — for The Goon Shows set a whole new trend in British humour, no question about that. I'm not a particularly nostalgic person but I tell you, mate, I still hanker for those days.'

Nostalgic or not, there is certainly some compelling force that drives him to look to the past for some of the answers to life in general and his own in particular. Although his childhood was not particularly happy he has been known to make pilgrimages to houses where he has lived or digs he stayed in, knock on the door and politely ask permission to look around. It is as if he might absorb something significant from the atmosphere, some clue as to what motivates him. Perhaps it is simply that he wants to relive the past, for he is on record as saying, 'the journey can often be more exhilarating, more fun, more exciting than reaching the destination.'

Sellers is a great believer in extra-sensory perception, and he is not alone in thinking he is psychic. After the war and up until she died Sellers frequently consulted Estelle Roberts, the distinguished medium. She it was who confirmed that one of the guiding forces in his life was the comedian Dan Leno who died in 1904. Sellers said recently, 'Leno is a very influential help in my career. He inspires me and fills my subconscious thought channels quite frequently.' Sellers even made a film 'The Optimist of Nine Elms' which is based on Leno.

Sellers does not talk about people dying, and when he says 'passed on' the words come naturally. He believes in reincarnation and is therefore extremely susceptible to atmosphere. So much so that he once said that if he visited the Colisseum he would imagine he had been there before as a martyred Christian. Daniel Mendoza of course figured prominently in fashioning his career, and also the clown Grimaldi. He is still in touch with his mother and he swears they are not imaginary conversations. Interestingly, Michael

Bentine is also deeply interested in paranormal phenomena.

Sellers first went to Estelle Roberts when he wanted to contact Larry Stephens who did some work on the early Goon Shows. The celebrated medium was unable to reach Stephens by name, but she was able to assure Sellers that he was contactable through the name of Fred. That name began to play a prominent part in Sellers' life and was instrumental for the 'Fred' shows. He even had a house called 'St Fred's'.

For a man who had such a Bedouin existence as a child it is difficult to appreciate why Sellers has moved so often. One would have thought he would want to put down permanent roots. Instead he has constantly been on the move: mansions, country cottages, penthouses, hotel suites ... Perhaps he is seeking the ideal home?

Like Milligan he admits to being a perfectionist, but unlike Spike he realizes that anyone who seeks that unattainable target is doomed to disappointment. Therefore one can never imagine Sellers cracking up mentally. He has too many distracting outlets. To date he has owned more than one hundred automobiles and a mere listing of a few of them reads like a catalogue for the Motor Show. He's owned all types of Jaguar, two Rolls-Royces, a Bentley Continental, Mercedes, Ferrari, Aston Martin, two Cadillacs, two Buicks, a Bristol Viotti, a Mini that cost more than a Rolls, plus an ambulance complete with a bed in the back. Sometimes he has kept a car for as little as a week. The one he has had the longest is the ancient Austin 12 tourer which he has restored to mint condition. It is the old jalopy he and The Goons careered through the West End in. At times his search for the ideal car has had near-disastrous consequences for his friends. Once when driving a new Jaguar he thought he heard a rattle and asked his friend Graham Stark to help him locate it. Stark listened intently, then expressed the view that it was coming from the boot. Obligingly he clambered in while Sellers drove around and he attempted to pin-point the fault. Unfortunately, during the drive Sellers spotted a business acquaintance, stopped the car and went for coffee, completely

Some of Peter Sellers' myriad film roles. *Top* Shop steward Fred Kite in *I'm All Right Jack; left* Major Robinson in *Soft Beds and Hard Battles; right* sadist Lionel Meadows in *Never Let Go.*

Top left A barrister in *A Case for the Jury; top right* A busker in *The Optimists; bottom left* a psychiatrist in *What's New Pussycat?; bottom right* General Latour in *Soft Beds and Hard Battles.*

Above Sellers has often consulted clairvoyant Maurice Woodruff before making big decisions. *Below* The 1962 Film Command Performance.

With his children Michael and Sarah.

With second wife Britt Ekland, in their Hollywood home, after his series of heart attacks.

With third wife Miranda Quarry after her illness.

Sellers, serious for once, holds an airstrip prayer meeting with guru before showering Belfast with peace leaflets.

forgetting the actor in the closed boot. It was only much later on his way home that Sellers heard the desperate hammering in the boot and remembered Stark. He swung off the road and opened the boot, just in time to let out a waxen-faced, near breathless, Stark.

The quest for perfection is also expressed in his constant buying of camera equipment, and he has been known to hop on a plane and fly to Switzerland to buy the latest item. To a minor extent it is also revealed in his love of gadgets and gimmicks. Like the cars, they often have a short-lived attraction. The life-size mechanical elephant lies neglected in some forgotten store room, the vast miniature railway that once filled an upstairs room has long been dismantled. A removal man recalled how once, when he and some mates were shifting Sellers' goods to a new home, the actor gave them a huge assortment of toys and sporting equipment. Some of it was brand new.

Although Sellers is not a religious man in the orthodox sense, he believes in a code of conduct that is basically Christian. 'I realize that God is everywhere around us and it is not necessary to worship in any big place in an organized way. I don't believe in doing down my neighbour, and I believe that people who do get punished for it by God,' he once told David Lewin, that doyen of entertainment writers. It was said with humility, not arrogance. For the past eight years he has found spiritual contentment in the study and practice of Hata Yoga. 'Yoga,' he said, 'appeals to me because it is completely free of dogmas and embraces all religions. I should know. I have been tutored in them all.'

Some people have accused Sellers of being indifferent to the fate of the human race, not on the grounds that he doesn't care but because there's nothing anyone can do about it. It is an unfair and false picture as one small incident shows. Sellers was riding in his chauffeur-driven Rolls over the 90-ft high viaduct which spans Highgate Hill and is known as 'suicide bridge', when he saw a man perched on the parapet threatening to jump.

He stopped the car and introduced himself: 'I am Peter Sellers, the actor.'

The man muttered a brusque, '.... off' and prepared to end it all.

Sellers promptly proceeded to give him a one man show. 'I gave him everything from The Goon Show to Doctor Strangelove and an imitation of Pat O'Brien's Irish-American brogue.' He kept up the non-stop patter and mimicry until the man's distraught wife arrived on the scene and managed to coax him down. Sellers' action was hardly that of a man indifferent to the fate of his fellow humans. On other occasions he has stopped and handed over a quid to someone down on their luck – and walked away without saying who he was.

On the professional side he doesn't have the hang-up about the role of the clown in society that Milligan has, and he saw no deep-rooted sociological significance in The Goon Shows. With remarkable candour he told the Cambridge University Indian Society – which was probably expecting a deep intellectual interpretation – that the Goons was 'a pleasant and illogical form of escapism. Some people try to make more out of it than is sometimes there.'

Career-wise he sees his future as a character actor; there is no clown bursting to play Hamlet. When Olivier asked him to play Lear at the Chichester Festival he turned it down. 'I'd always said I wouldn't do Shakespeare. I suppose I might have done one of the clowns, but I don't want to do a clown.'

Sellers simply wants to be a character actor streets ahead of anybody else; a lot of people say he already is, but he still thinks there is a lot of talent as yet untapped. Apart from that his approach to life is now simple and uncomplicated. 'I'm an absolutely normal person, lucky to be earning a good living – extravagant because I never have known the value of money – and I don't care a row of beans as long as my family are cared for and I'm not penniless when I'm sixty. I don't believe in being the richest man in the cemetery. That's my philosophy.'

Chapter Seven

COURT JESTERS

From time immemorial there has always been room in the royal courts for the clown. Long before monarchs had discovered the importance of hygiene and floors were strewn with rushes and unwanted bones were kicked about until lost, the therapeutic value of laughter as an outlet to lift the burden of state affairs was recognized. The cap-and-bells jester with a pig's bladder at the end of a stick was as essential to enlightened rule as any sycophantic minister. It took a wise man to play the fool. Victoria, not renowned for her propensity for amusement, was known to have occasionally summoned laughter makers to her presence to lift the pall of gloom that so often shrouded her court. Her son Edward VII was the complete opposite and demanded constant entertainment. Dan Leno, the darling of the London music halls, and much much later Peter Sellers' spiritual lodestar, was often commanded by the King to provide after-dinner laughter at Sandringham.

Leno, the stage name of George Galvin (1861–1904), like Sellers came from a theatrical background, and apart from being the world's champion clog-dancer, he had a brand of humour that was years ahead of its time and which particularly appealed to the *bon viveur* sovereign. Leno, who was born in London's Somers Town, has even been compared to the Goons. For in his stage patter he talked of a girl who 'winked at me with her ear' and of a voice 'thick with passion and bulging at both ends'.

Alas, as with Mendoza, royal patronage wasn't the *open sesame* to wealth and status. He died when he was forty-three, broken in mind and body, deeply mourned by London's working folk but barely missed by those members of Society who had once felt flattered to be in his company.

Later, the Crazy Gang became the unofficial court jesters

and no Royal Command Variety Performance was complete without the badinage that was aimed at the Royal Box. But while the Crazy Gang took minor liberties and aimed some of their cracks directly at their tiara'ed patrons, the humour was always kept well in check, never overstepped the mark, and was invariably respectful. There was no undue familiarity. Even so, it was considered very forward by many fuddy-dudders who felt it smacked of *lèse majesté*. The Crazy Gang were never allowed to hang a 'By Appointment' sign outside their dressing rooms, and the Royal Family did not go out of their way to enthuse about them. It wasn't the done thing to establish close relationships with entertainers.

The Goons altered all that by establishing close personal links with members of the Royal Family. It was something that had never happened before and until another team establishes a similar rapport it is extremely unlikely to happen again. It is more than just the easing of protocol in a modern society or part of a calculated attempt to improve the royal image and make the Royal Family less remote. The Royals really are Goon addicts. And they admit it with unfettered enthusiasm.

Prince Philip, never one to suffer fools gladly, even chose The Goons as his champions to play against the Cambridge University Tiddlywinks Club. The late Duchess of Kent was a devotee and, with her daughter Princess Alexandra attended more than one Goon recording. Princess Anne has unwound enough to simulate hoofbeats with coconut shells at a Goon Show while Princess Margaret and Lord Snowdon have long been ardent fans. Peter Sellers has been seen in their company so often now that he can be considered one of the members of the privileged 'Set'.

But the greatest accolade of all must be in the confession of the Prince of Wales who said that it was a matter of profound regret to him that he was not born earlier than 1948 so that he wouldn't have missed the pleasures of the early Goon Shows. Unfortunately, he said, they were drawing to an end when he became a member of their fan club. But he did listen to some of the shows under the protective cover of his bedclothes when he was a pupil at Gordonstoun.

Royalty has certainly moved closer to the people in recent years, but even those people who would like to see them riding through the streets on bicycles were impressed when their heir to the Throne went so far as to write a foreword to a book of *Goon Show Scripts*.

At one time it would have been unheard of, even undreamed of, for the Prince of Wales to write a foreword to a commercial publication, let alone rhapsodize in terms of charming familiarity about the talents of the people involved. He used the kind of words usually reserved for people who are writing about Royalty, not vice-versa. That is no criticism, for while it did The Goons a lot of good it also elevated the Prince in the eyes of the public who were more than delighted to see he had a will and taste of his own, and wasn't going to be deterred from saying what he wanted to say. The man in the street doesn't see or care when eyebrows are raised admonishingly in important places. As for the Prince, he has made personal appearances on the stage and made a first class job of it. He had a perfect right to speak as one entertainer to three others. He has even appeared on stage in a dustbin.

The Prince's foreword, written on Buckingham Palace notepaper, talked of The Goons' humour appealing to him 'with an hysterical totality' and he regretted that he hadn't savoured the 'unbounded joy of listening avidly to The Goons' during the early shows because he wasn't old enough.

He confessed that he knew the Ying Tong Song by heart – the only one he does know – and that he sang it to his younger brothers together with 'Solo for a Raspberry Blower'. It says a lot for his powers of mimicry, for when his brothers heard The Goon Show for the first time they thought it was Prince Charles.

Claiming to be one of their 'dotty and devoted' supporters, he hoped there would be more and more scripts and records published over the years as they brought such pleasure to countless fans whose devotion demonstrated the 'eternal quality of Goon humour'.

The Prince could even joke about the amount of money the book would make and refer to the 'leek eating Welshman called Secombe who has committed the unforgivable sin of *lèse majesté*.'

He concluded, 'This is not a reference to an indolent Gallic Monarch, but stems from his cry of "Eccles for King!" "There's many a true word spoken in jest", so they say, so beware Milligan, Sellers, Secombe and Co. . . .'

Far from being shocked the public were delighted with his literary debut. Imagine Victoria's reaction if Edward had written in similar terms about Dan Leno! Prince Charles was on safe ground anyway, for his enthusiasm is shared by most of his family.

The association is remarkable in more ways than one, for the Royal Family, always careful to tread the tightrope between undue stuffiness and undue familiarity, has never been criticized for the closeness of their friendship with The Goons. There have, however, been some carping criticisms of The Goons from a fistful of people who think they have overstepped the mark and embarrassed them. But as they haven't been 'dropped' one can only assume that the Royal Family took it all in good part.

The most outspoken accusation of bad taste was levelled at Peter Sellers when he made a recording with Anthony Newley in New York called 'Fool Britannia' which centred around the still-fresh Profumo Scandal that came perilously close to toppling Mr Harold Macmillan's government. Before an audience which included Vivien Leigh, Sammy Davis junior, Stanley Baker and Richard Burton's first wife Sybil, Sellers and Newley produced an LP record that satirized British reaction to the scandal which led to the resignation of the War Minister John Profumo who lied about his association with Christine Keeler.

Anthony Carthew, the New York correspondent for the long-since departed *Daily Herald*, the official organ of the TUC, was surprisingly the most appalled. 'I might as well tell you that I am sure it will be banned in Britain, since well over half its items seem to be to be either libellous, or breaches of privilege. The rest are just plain dirty.

'There is one item which might even be treason, and could result in Sellers and Newley being sent to the Tower, if the Beefeaters are not on strike at the time.'

Sellers did a brilliant skit of Premier Harold Macmillan defending Britain's security services to the House of Commons, but that was considered fair game. Macmillan could retaliate if he wanted to; the Monarch couldn't if she were the subject of a lampooning sketch.

Carthew wrote, 'I have reservation about a Buckingham Palace scene (Sellers as the female voice) which is mostly rather nasty innuendo only slightly redeemed by lines like "We are at home now dear, you don't have to keep on smiling and waving."

'And: "Anne, how many times have I told you not to ride your pony on the tea table?" '

Not surprisingly there were follow-up stories saying that the long-playing record which satirized the Royal Family, the Prime Minister and British morality would be banned in England. The Decca organization refused to handle it on the grounds that it was 'in bad taste', and Newley was forced to issue it himself. Sellers said, 'Only a prude could possibly be offended by it,' and added, 'I am quite sure that Prince Philip would get a good laugh out of it.'

When in fact the record was released it hardly caused a ripple of disapproval. If any criticism can be levelled at Sellers it was his lack of tact, because the Profumo Affair had caused a lot of resentment against the Establishment and satirizing the Royal Family at a time when they were aware of the criticisms was not particularly kind or generous. Sellers had also left himself open to the charge that he was trading on his friendship, because he was known to be friendly with Princess Margaret and Lord Snowdon, and had even made a humorous home-movie with the Queen's sister taking part. But that suggestion can be dismissed out of hand. Many of his friends will readily talk about his shortcomings but they do not include malice, while his regard for friendships is too intense for him to risk losing them.

As his friend Herbert Kretzmer put it, 'The great thing about Peter is that he is a lovable man. You love him despite everything, you love him in many ways because of his almost tragic shortcomings.'

When Sellers expressed surprise at the storm of protest, he was being genuine and certainly not glib. Throughout his distinguished career he had mimicked many close friends and based film characters on real life people who raised no objections, so it probably never occurred to him that anyone could take offence at a bit of leg-pulling.

If the Royal Family were displeased they certainly made no attempt to let it be known, and in fact an opportunity arose some years later when they could have administered a regal snub. They didn't, they laughed uproariously.

It arose on the occasion of the Queen's 39th birthday when Princess Margaret took the Queen, Prince Philip, Prince Charles, Princess Anne, Lord Snowdon and Peter Sellers and his wife Britt, along to see Milligan in 'Son of Oblomov'. It wasn't a surprise descent on the theatre, Milligan had been forewarned, but that didn't deter him from some very personal ad-libbing. He walked to the footlights and in true red-nose comic style shouted, 'I say, I say, is there a Peter Sellers in the house?'

Sellers, sitting with the Royal party called back, 'Yes, there is a Peter Sellers in the house,' in the voice of the straight 'feed' man. And so started an astonishing cross patter between the two former Goons. The audience loved it and the newspapers seized on every verbal exchange between the two comics and noted how the Royal Family had wholeheartedly joined in the fun.

Milligan shouted, 'Why does Prince Philip wear red, white and blue braces?' and Sellers his stooge dutifully responded, 'I don't know, why does Prince Philip wear red, white and blue braces?' Milligan replied, 'To keep his trousers up.'

It wasn't the most scintillating exchange and one suspects the laughter was only so hilarious because the Royal Family were involved. More than one third rate comedian has been given the bird for such antiquated exchanges as:

Milligan: Why can't a lady with a wooden leg change a pound note?

Sellers: I don't know. Why can't a lady with a wooden leg change a pound note?

Milligan: Because she's only got half a knicker.

When Spike leapt on to a bed with a girl from the cast he shouted, 'Philip, get that lad of yours out of here.'

Some people have claimed that the Queen was not particularly amused but had no alternative except to laugh. Disapproval on her part would have been highly embarrassing for all concerned. Such comments are often made by people who like to give the impression that they are 'in' with the Royal Family.

Whatever the truth, it did not prevent Sellers and his wife and Milligan and his wife being invited back for dinner.

And judging from Spike's own account it was a very informal and homely meal. More surprising was the fact that Milligan, the scourge of the Establishment, was completely captivated.

He drove with his wife to Kensington Palace in his battered Mini with odd pieces of string dangling down, and was almost lost for words when Princess Margaret said, 'Come over and meet my sister.' The not normally tongue-tied Spike didn't know what to talk about. When he glanced around the room and spotted some toys – a teddy bear, a child's rocking chair and a horse's head – lying around, he decided to engage the Queen in a conversation about his children. Together they exchanged their views on how a family should be brought up, and Milligan explained how he was most anxious not to stifle their imaginative instincts. The comic was totally disarmed by the naturalness of the Queen and went on to tell her how concerned he was that his children should be able to enjoy fantasy as well as the harsh realities of life. Spike in full spate described how he left fairy notes on the lawn for them to find, all enclosed in fairy envelopes with fairy stamps. They contained formal little announcements such as, 'The fairy Queen has had a baby. We have put it in a walnut shell.' He spellbound his children, he explained, with delightful stories about full moon dances on the kitchen table and banquets which began with dandelion soup. Apart from the make-believe he wanted his children to share his own sense of wonderment in nature; an insect was not just a minute dot but a living creature beautifully proportioned and created.

The Queen in turn talked quite naturally about the special problems of bringing up her own family and emerged in Milligan's eyes as a humane person much concerned with motherly problems and not just a remote symbol.

Milligan had been told in advance of the invitation and his three children had each sent along a birthday present of a book and a comic strip and self-portraits they had written and painted themselves. It was a warm gesture of the kind that children make with such spontaneity, and the Queen was delighted.

Spike, with astonishing lack of foresight, had turned up wearing a grey lounge suit, and his Gunners Tie, to find the other men wearing dinner jackets. Prince Philip immediately put him at his ease by drawing attention to the tie and opening a conversation about the services. And he revealed that when it came to the quick quip he was a match for Spike's repartee. 'I hope, sir', said Milligan, 'you weren't with one of those British warships that used to fire on us when we were flying to and fro between North Africa and Italy?'

'No, Spike,' he replied, 'we had a very polite crew. They never fired on anybody.'

When they eventually sat down to dinner, Spike was sat next to Princess Margaret who served the saddle of lamb herself. Later the Queen cut her own birthday cake and passed the pieces round. Milligan with his working class background couldn't get over the fact that the Queen and Princess Margaret didn't have uniformed flunkeys waiting to jump at the slightest hint of a crooked finger.

Apart from underlining just how far the Royal Family have moved away from the stiff and starchy protocol-bound life of not-too-far-distant monarchs – at one stage they wouldn't have been seen at a race meeting with a divorcee – it emphasized the closeness of their association with the two Goons. It was after all an intimate family occasion.

Earlier Sellers had sent a warning telegram to Milligan saying there must be no Goonery over the dinner table, and Spike adhered to that. It was Prince Philip who got the laughs by setting fire to the table cloth while trying to do a Tommy Cooper act. The Prince calmly put out the fire with a jug of water.

When the meal was over and they retired to the drawing room, Sellers and Milligan staged an impromptu cabaret. Sellers exhumed an old act he used to do in his RAF days, and took off Tod Slaughter that master of Grand Guignol playing Sweeney Todd the Demon Barber of Fleet Street. 'I wish the world was one big throat and I had the cutting of it,' he roared, as he leered and hammed his way through the story of the man who made the best meat pies in London. It was hilarious barn-storming stuff and the royal party thoroughly enjoyed it as he deliberately muffed his lines and ad-libbed with a few of his own jokes.

Together he and Milligan repeated some of the pre-Goon Show warm-up material, then slipped into the routine of two Scotsmen who begin to fight a duel with swords, circling and snarling at each other before ending up with their weapons lying crossed on the floor all ready for a Highland dance. The imaginary curtain came down with them standing back to back, then walking away, and turning at the end of ten carefully measured paces to shoot each other.

Princess Margaret applauded and confessed, 'I always feel nostalgic about The Goons. They are part of our generation.' Prince Charles was laughing louder than anybody. Later when Milligan sent him a recording of the celebrated 'The Starlings' he got a reply from Gordonstoun signed simply Charles in which the heir apparent wrote saying how he and his friends used to listen to the later Goon Shows after lights out. This incidentally was the show in which the Queen was mimicked.

'I must say,' said Milligan, 'I liked the boy. He reminded

155

me of my own son Sean. He was quiet and he had this wonderful gift which mere position cannot give you, a sense of
humour. It is comforting to me to feel that when he comes
to sit on the throne we shall have a man who also knows how
to laugh.' A rave notice from a self-confessed Marxist-
Catholic whose politics and view of life are hardly on the side
of the Establishment.

Perhaps it was the naturalness which most impressed him.
Not that it was his first encounter with royalty. Neither was
it the first occasion when he had found them to be far
removed from the image presented in the Court Circulars.
Once, just before a Goon Show recording at the Camden
Theatre, Milligan was surprised to learn that the Duke of
Kent, Princess Marina, and Princess Alexandra had turned up
unexpectedly. Milligan suggested they all adjourn to the bar
for a drink, and ignorant or forgetful, of protocol, he went
in ahead of the royal party saying, 'Follow me.' Having done
something which a few years previous would have made headline news, he asked Princess Alexandra if she didn't get
bored with all the protocol. The Princess replied, 'Yes, we
could do with a little less of it. We're all much more normal
than we're allowed to be. But the protocol goes ahead of us
and, when we arrive, we're surrounded by it.'

Milligan so far is the only one of the trio who has not been
honoured. Both Sellers and Secombe have been awarded the
CBE.

Secombe has also been invited to an informal lunch at Buckingham Palace which he considers one of the most memorable
occasions in his life. He recalls that when he and his wife were
introduced to the Queen and Prince Philip he was still wearing
side-boards for his role in 'Pickwick'. But apart from repeating
Prince Philip's crack, 'Hullo! I've heard about five o'clock
shadow but this is ridiculous,' he has kept a modest and
discreet silence about the meeting.

He has, however, unstinting admiration for Prince Charles
both as a man, humorist and Goon fan. When Prince Charles
reviewed his first novel *Twice Brightly* for *Punch* and
described it as a 'compendium of Welsh wit and thespianism'

Secombe said he considered him the best critic in the history of book selling.

Sellers, a photographer of skill and imagination, has been invited to take official photographs of the Queen Mother and Prince Charles; a rare accolade from a family which can boast one of the country's top photographers.

Another example of the unique rapport that exists is when Sellers took Princess Margaret to Ronnie Scott's jazz club one night and Scott read out a couplet sent by Milligan who should have been there but couldn't make it. It said, 'Wherever you are, wherever you be, please take your hand off the Princess's knee.'

The newspapers printed it together with a picture of Sellers and Princess Margaret leaving the club, and there wasn't one indignant reader's letter.

There will always be the odd carper who would prefer the Royal Family to remain in an ivory tower, but for the vast majority of people the new trend has served to make them warmer and much more flesh-and-blood persons instead of remote figureheads. And far from diminishing the public's affection and loyalty, it has only served to increase it.

It is also a tremendous tribute to The Goons that they have established close links with the Royal Family and it shows how truly classless is their humour. When Prince Charles wrote of 'the eternal quality of Goon humour' he was the spokesman for millions of families, for few comics have bridged the generation gap so completely that Mum, Dad and the children all share The Goons' sense of fun with equal enthusiasm and understanding.

Chapter Eight

THE GOONS' RETURN

There is no sadder spectacle in the world of public entertainment than the performer who cashes in on a 'positively last performance' with regularly staged return appearances.

Some artists, particularly in the operatic sphere, have tarnished what otherwise would have been immortal reputations by their unwillingness to depart the scene. The flat notes are more remembered than the perfectly hit high C's. Some just cannot accept that the curtain must come down at some time or other. Vanity or avarice prompts them to stage just one more come back, until they become laughing stocks and the brunt of bar-room barbs. A dozen names spring to mind, but in deference to their memory they shall remain unwritten.

Sellers, Milligan and Secombe were determined that The Goon Shows should not go on until they became one big yawn. They deliberately decided to call it a day. True, there were problems in getting the three much-in-demand stars together every Sunday, but that wasn't the main obstacle. They had reached the stage where they had begun to feel that you *can* have too much of a good thing. The final programme, 'The Last Smoking Seagoon', was transmitted on 28th January, 1960, when they were at their peak and their fans would have accepted a breakfast, luncheon and dinner diet of Goonery. If the trio had not achieved such individual success they might, perhaps, not have been so resolute in their determination. Certainly there was no financial incentive to make them want to keep it going; money was the least of their problems. But it's a wise champion who retires with the crown still on his head, and that's how The Goons saw the situation. They were determined that what had filled such a happy and rewarding period in their lives should not end on a note of soured disillusionment.

It was all summed up by Sellers, who admitted that while The Goon period had been the most contented in his career, it was time to ring down the curtain. 'I don't want to be a Goon all my life ... The Goons can't hang together much longer. In fact, I can't see it lasting this series. We've had six years of it, and we've had a bellyful ... It's got to end sometime.'

That was as early as 1956 and, in fact, the series went on for several more years, but it showed that Sellers had already seen the writing on the wall. When the irrevocable decision was taken it wasn't because staleness or boredom had set in; it was simply that their professional instincts rang an alarm bell. As John Browell put it, 'The break-up was inevitable. As a producer I very much believe in stopping something before the public get tired of it. There's nothing worse than "Oh! Not again." Although the public still wanted more, it was a deliberate and wise decision to end it. The job of making people laugh week after week requires an incredible effort. It consumes people. For me it was one of the most successful periods in my life, but I was emotionally involved in the programme and that leaves scars.'

There were no recriminations, no regrets, and everyone remained friends. But having made the decision The Goons found they just couldn't turn their backs on Eccles, Bloodnok and company. The lovable monsters they had created refused to obey the stage direction Exit. They continued to meet regularly for lunch, dinner, and social get-togethers, where they immediately reverted to Goonery and lapsed into their favourite impersonations. The meetings resembled those hilarious warm-up sessions which preceded the shows.

No matter where they were, and all three did a fair amount of globe-trotting, they continued to write each other crazy letters and postcards, and spend a small fortune on delightfully loony telegrams. Sometimes a cable would contain no more than 'Fire', or 'Help'. Often their zany sense of the ridiculous wasn't always appreciated, as when Secombe was flying abroad and the police received an anonymous telegram warning them to keep watch at the airport for a man masquerading as the famous comedian Harry Donald Secombe. The police swooped, and Harry had a difficult five minutes convincing them that he wasn't an impostor. But once he showed them his passport and emitted the famous giggle, all was well. All wide-eyed innocence he assured them he had no idea who the anonymous sender could be.

All three are talented cartoonists and their twenty years long war of correspondence has been enhanced by their sketches, caricatures and doodles. They even went to the length of having special headed paper printed for some of

159

their letters. Sellers invented a firm of solicitors who specialized in oaths and threats; Milligan had a firm of chemists and abortionists. Certainly over the years they have made a big personal contribution to the Post Office's never-ending battle for solvency.

There were telegrams about socks from Cardinal Wolsey, cheques made out in Moriarty money, beautifully etched 'real money' banknotes, and long poems in the excruciating style of McGonnagall, the world's worst bard. A thanks for lunch card would carry a P.S. – 'See you during the next hunger period.' Milligan once received a telegram: 'Move one degree repeat and watch my mess tin next time – Angry Jim.' From America Sellers wrote to Spike an official looking paper informing him that he had just purchased shares in a North Pole coconut farm, from a certain Major Denis Bloodnok. Another telegrammed gem of wisdom said: 'There is no justice as the prisoner remarked when the court convened without a judge.' The constant exchange of letters, cards and telegrams provided enough material to produce a best-seller, *The Book of The Goons*. But the war of words didn't start with any kind of publication in mind; it was all spontaneous, rib-nudging fun, and purely personal: no one gave a thought to cashing in on it. And its continuation was simply a means of not completely severing the umbilical chord. In some magical way the letters and odd meetings replaced those deeply missed Sundays. They were being let out of school. Often the exchanges reflected the grass roots of Goon Humour; an odd item of news would plant the seed of an idea which yesteryear would have resulted in a script.

Milligan, who had just received from Sellers a press-cutting about an American mayor who had conducted a massive search for his lost false teeth and found them up a telegraph pole, scoured the papers for a suitable rejoinder and settled for an item which detailed at great length a new Anglo-Saxon method for counting sheep.

When Secombe spoke to Spike on the telephone after being out of touch for some considerable time, Milligan wrote back demanding a refund of the £2 he had forked out towards a wreath for Harry, who had been 'missing presumed dead'.

As Harry explained, 'We might not see each other for ages but when we do it's instant hysteria. It's a chemistry that never fails to work.'

They did attempt to recapture the magic of the old Goon days with twenty-six fifteen-minute puppet shows titled 'The Telegoons', in 1963, and although the same old wonderful characters were exhumed and the Goon-starved fans loved it, the show somehow missed the bull's-eye. The Goons didn't really transfer to television. Ironically the radio shows they had managed to make so visual didn't have the same impact on the 'box'. Everyone had their own private, mental picture of the various characters as actual people, and the puppet figures were too artificial and manipulated. It's an interesting aspect of The Goons' magnetism that when the BBC invited listeners to send in drawings of what they thought the major characters looked like nearly all of them bore a striking similarity. Eccles, Bluebottle, Moriarty ... all conjured up visual portraits that were not widely different. The vital thing was that the mind-pictures lived and breathed, whereas those hand-made puppets didn't.

After that experience it is more than likely that The Goons would have become no more than a nostalgic memory, and a subject for after-dinner reminiscing, if it hadn't been for the need to commemorate an historic moment in the life of the BBC. In 1972, Aunty Beeb notched up her fiftieth birthday and plans were laid down for a series of programmes that would mirror the organization's achievements. It was also an opportunity to show how the BBC had progressed with the times. And what better proof could there be than to get The Goons together again? A programme that for so long had been given the thumbs-down signal because of its too-advanced sense of humour, would not only be welcomed back but it would show there was no room in the new BBC for the fuddy-duddy 'Let's-play-safe' attitude that marked the fifties.

And so on 30th April, 1972, The Goons came roaring back.

It was a tremendous tribute to Sellers, Secombe and Milligan to be asked to provide a programme in honour of half a century of radio broadcasting.

Twelve years had passed since their last broadcast together, and it was only natural that the venue for the 'return' should be the old Camden Theatre where the 'farewell' had taken place. It had also been the scene of some of their most brilliant shows. In pre-war days, the 'Old Camden' as it was known to North Londoners was a place where you queued and paid a 'tanner' to see second-time-around movies. On that famous night the crocodile outside the box office would not have been out of place at the Old Vic or the Opera House Covent Garden. It was an 'in' occasion.

The calendar was flipped back as if there had never been a break, and the warm-up session before the show proper was as daft and unpredictable as ever. The Press was there in force to record a joke-by-joke account of the momentous return which had begun to assume General MacArthur proportions in the eyes of the British public. Peter Sellers in steel-rimmed bins stood on his head for the photographers, while Milligan explained, 'This is for the Australian papers.'

The questions flew and the pencils frantically squiggled Pitman outlines in an effort to keep pace with the non-stop flow of quips and asides.

'What is the plot?'

'We've never had one,' retorted Secombe.

Milligan angrily contradicted him: 'I've got a plot. It's in Golders Green Crematorium.'

Harry, eager to oblige, blew a classic Seagoon raspberry, followed by demoniacal giggles and a few bars of a ballad in which he managed to convince everybody that the old power and melodic qualities were still there, and ear plugs were the order of the day. The three clowned shamelessly. The air was filled with countless accents: guttural German officers, top bracket 'smoothy' civil servants, and gouty colonels.

The suave velvet voice of George 'my dear fellow' Sanders

was contradicted by an Indian gentleman. The querulous tones of Crun broke up the threatened argument. Minnie Bannister sided with her wrinkled paramour.

It was all just like old times. Twelve years were blown away in a gale of mirth. Except that Harry had a couple more chins, Sellers was thinner, and Milligan a little greyer. Otherwise the time barrier had been demolished as effectively as if Doctor Who had had a hand in stage-managing it.

There was more than a hint of sadness in the air too. The Camden Theatre was scheduled for demolition.

Buried under a non-stop avalanche of questions, Sellers decided to be serious for the whole length of the time it took him to say, 'Come back? It doesn't feel as though we've been away. You know, our humour was really way ahead of its time. All those satire boys, "Beyond the Fringe", "Private Eye", they took on what we started.'

Outside the queue stretched like a piece of elastic perilously near breaking point. The BBC ticket department had been so inundated with applications that the 500-seat theatre could have been filled ten times over. There was no possible hope of the majority of them getting in, but years of Goon idolatry had instilled in them an incurable optimism. The black-market in tickets turned Camden Town into Wembley on Cup Final day. People who were in a position to pull a few strings were still out in the cold, but, somehow or other, the 'spivs' had managed to get their hands on tickets which were available at £15 each.

The tickets were originally allocated with scrupulous fairness, but a privileged handful had no trouble in getting seats. Long established and ardent Goon fans had been the first on the list. Not that they would have been locked out if they had turned up at the last minute. No one would have had the temerity to hold up 'house full' notices to the Duke of Edinburgh, Princess Anne, Princess Margaret or Lord Snowdon – anyway, he was there in his official capacity as a Press photographer.

The keenest fan of the lot had been unable to make it. He was all at sea, as Sellers might have put it. Prince Charles

163

on duty with HMS *Norfolk*, a guided-missile destroyer, had cabled ruefully: 'Last night my hair fell out and my knees dropped off with envy when I thought of my father and sister attending the show.'

Ex-RAF physical training instructor Ray Ellington, the loose-limbed coloured musician-singer and leader of the famous quartet which bore his name, was back in harness and doubling as Ellinga, batman to Bloodnok. Max Geldray, the Dutch-born harmonica player, had been specially flown in from California where he was working for the Christian Science Movement. The printed programme described him as, 'Dutch nose swinger and harmonica player extraordinaire'. John Browell found himself back in the role of producer with the near-impossible task of curbing the Goons' exuberance. The family reunion was almost complete. For sentimental reasons the recording was made on a Sunday night, although the show proper was not due to be relayed until October.

Finally the dummy runs were over, the red and green studio lights flashed the warning that the recording was about to start. Milligan, Sellers and Secombe took up their positions by the microphones. The Goons were back in business. As the flood gates of memory were opened it seemed as if they had only been away for a short tea break.

The announcer solemnly pronounced, 'As everybody who read the Isle of Arran Shoemaker's Monthly knows, Her Majesty the Queen was to have opened a Goon Show, but owing to a nasty rumour called Grocer Heath she has declined. However, at short notice and wearing a floral cretonne frock, Mr Secombe has agreed to stand in for His Sovereign.'

Glasses perched precariously on his nose like a tipsy parrot clinging to its perch, a puffing, giggling Harry now bellowed into the microphone like a prize fight announcer: 'Ladeez'n Genelmen, my first impression as Queen will be a hedgehog doing an acupuncture on Yul Brynner's nut.'

The Royal Party were in stitches. It was even better than the ad-libbed asides they still remembered from 'Son of Oblomov'. Nothing had changed. The incorrigible trio knew there was no dark dungeon awaiting them at The Tower –

there might have been if they had been deferential and patronizing.

Seconds later Secombe was on again at Sellers: 'Haven't you read the Court Circular?' – 'No, I'm waiting till they've made the film.'

The auditorium was suddenly filled with the clip-clop-clip of hoof beats, and Secombe, hand cupped over one ear, said in his Queen's voice, 'That sounds like me and my description of running up the M1 to Blackpool, played by my daughter.'

The announcer had interrupted to proclaim in an official-sounding voice: 'The coconuts were played at short notice by a young lady from Buckingham Palace.' And it was no leg pull. Princess Anne, at her father's instigation, had taken over the coconut shells for the sound effects men.

Vincent Mulchrone of the *Daily Mail* wrote: 'But apart from tilts at the Royal box, which was tilting with laughter itself, it was the old Goon Show, the purist form of surrealist humour on radio – or "talking-type wireless" as The Goons still prefer to call it.

'They were all there, unchanged, instant immortals – the whining Bluebottle ("You filthy rotten swine you") along with public school conman Hercules Gryptype-Thynne, Major Bloodnok and quavery Henry Crun – all played by Sellers.

'Secombe was back to Neddy Seagoon and Milligan was the key figure Eccles, the dimwit with the voice akin to Disney's Goofy.

'Peter Sellers told me, "It's like a strange dream. As if we never parted." '

Mulchrone, an avid Goon-fan and no mean humorist himself, was moved by the wave of nostalgia that had engulfed the studio, while Sellers' remark which hinted at some para-normal continuity prompted him to reflect: 'Strange indeed ... The Miracle was that in just eight hours of rehearsal yesterday they became the Goons again, sparkling and crackling, ad libbing to try to "throw" each other, changing lines in a flash, giving the old appearance of enjoying themselves even more than the audience.

'It seemed to come naturally to them. In truth, it did.

As Harry Secombe put it: "Our degree of sophistication never was any more than fingernail deep anyway."'

Their humour had the same old simplicity, coupled with that indefinable touch of magic which defied copying.

'How do you open a door?'

'Turn the knob on your side.'

'I haven't got a knob on my side.'

'On the door!'

Without warning Spike had burst into San Francisco, except the words were different: 'I left my teeth on Table Mountain, high on a hill they smile at me...'

Mulchrone's wonderfully evocative review made it all sound so easy and natural. It was far from it as he explained recently when asked to recall that celebrated night. He had ended his article with these words: 'By midnight, after a bit of nosh with Royalty in the foyer of the old theatre where they recorded so many of their Shows, the Goons were back on their separate paths.

'Pity. With a bit of foresight we could have imprisoned them in a luxurious studio for life so that their unique idiocy could sustain us in a world gone crazy in quite a different way.'

Mulchrone was expressing what so many people felt. Without being too emotive, there were a lot of people who had not only shed a few tears, but had also lost a few years in age; like someone on a crash diet shedding unwanted poundage. It had been as emotional as looking at yesteryear's holiday snaps when the rain was forgotten and only the sunshine remembered.

The Royal Party had posed for pictures with Secombe, Sellers and Milligan. The question that was on everybody's lips was asked: 'What about more Goon shows?' – 'No, I think not,' Milligan had said. 'It was a once-only night. I'm ready for a wheelchair now.' There was an air of finality in his words.

Then the lights had dimmed in the theatre, the doors locked, while the crowds headed for home, the date of the actual broadcast indelibly registered in the diaries of their minds. (When it did go out there were several million young-sters who now knew at first hand what Mum and Dad were talking about when, with almost reverential tones, they dis-cussed The Goons.)

Next morning the newspapers had been filled with hun-dreds of column inches about the come-back and final farewell of The Goons. Under a splash banner-heading 'The Goon-powder Pot', the *Daily Express* carried a large picture of Milligan, Secombe and Sellers with Prince Philip, Princess Anne, Lord Snowdon and Princess Margaret, and announcing the date of the broadcast had said, 'If you're too young to know the Beatles, at least you'll be able to stop asking Daddy: Who *was* the famous Eccles?'

And of course when it was broadcast it all sounded so spontaneous and effortless that people just couldn't under-stand why The Goons wanted to call it a day. In fact, it hadn't all come naturally. It had been the result of a long hard slog that the public and the Royal visitors were unaware of.

When this chapter was being written, Vincent Mulchrone was asked what it was *really* like behind the scenes before the public were admitted to the studio. He said: 'The Goons had first got together in the afternoon to work over the script, and people like me had slipped in to watch the idiot geniuses at work. In the studio the technicians were falling about laughing at their jokes and antics. Then it was tea-time and a photocall. Like other daily newspapermen, I was fighting against time and I had a deadline to make, if I was to get it in the first edition. That meant I had to actually write it before the show-proper opened. I went off to the band re-hearsal room with a flask of Scotch and sat down to write. Then who should come in, of all people, but Milligan, Sellers and Secombe, and Lord Snowdon who wanted to take some pictures. They started going through the script again and Milligan began making massive changes. Ideas were flashing backwards and forwards and Spike was changing everything with maddening ferocity. I've been in some pretty tight situ-ations in various parts of the world, but nothing was quite so nerve bending as trying to write my piece and at the same time keeping one ear open for the alterations being made. I couldn't put jokes in my story that wouldn't be heard later. I was also helpless with laughter, and that didn't help things. When they saw my trouble they came over and helped me out. With half an hour to go they were still re-writing the script. It was quite as mad as that. I was really impressed by Milligan, that mad perfectionist, because the script was being improved line by line, word by word.'

Lord Snowdon captured the backstage tension with a series of superb pictures showing the three at work. Hunched over a plain table, and surrounded by metal lockers, the bespectacled trio revealed the serious side of humour. Only the bottle of Moet Chandon and the plastic cups revealed it as a night to remember and celebrate.

The reaction to the broadcast was tremendous. Millions tuned in and everyone was unanimous that the old magic was still there. When the show was issued as an LP record, so many copies were sold that it won a silver disc. More than 70,000 copies were bought. It showed there was still a tremendous market for their humour, but The Goons were adamant. Outside their private lives The Goons no longer existed.

Is there any chance of them changing their minds?

Chapter Nine

IN CLOSE-UP

O wad some Pow'r the giftie gie us
To see oursels as others see us!

So wrote the immortal Rabbie Burns with the heroic thought in mind that the world would be a better place if our strengths, weaknesses, foibles and frailties were ruthlessly exposed. On a less grandiose scale his sentiments apply equally when one is trying to create word portraits of individuals that are not merely veneer-deep.

Well, The Goons can't complain they have been ignored on any of those scores. No three people have been so meticulously examined under the public microscope – dissected, analysed, stretched on metaphorical couches, probed, questioned, laid bare and prodded.

And with an honesty that would have delighted the down-to-earth Burns, The Goons themselves have contributed thousands and thousands of words on how they see themselves and each other. A verbal dance of the seven veils, almost.

And the outcome?

Milligan and Sellers, the friends with a love-hate relationship, still emerge rather blurred images, like men whose portraits lack definition because the photographer had camera shake. Refusing to be tagged with convenient labels, they are – and will continue to be – enigmas. They remain annoyingly inconsistent even when writing or talking about themselves or each other.

Secombe is the exception. Unstintingly and uncritically admired by the other two, he emerges as the rock of the trio. Swopping the geological variety for the seaside one: bite anywhere along it and you get the same Harry Donald Secombe, who set out from Swansea full of hope and optimism, so many years ago. His sole sense of guilt is at being paid so much money for simply doing something he enjoys immensely.

There is, however, one thing about them which no one disputes: their Goon humour is unique, and lasting. But how do others see them, and their zany buffoonery? And, gifted now with 'the Pow'r' of hindsight, how do they see themselves?

Dennis Main Wilson, first producer of the Goon Show – he goes back to the Grafton Arms nights – believes Goonery was a product of the times and born out of the almost hysterical euphoria which swept Britain after the last war.

Wilson, a serious student of humour, says, 'Great humour always reflects the mood of the times and The Goons did just that. Because of the war, we had become men together at the same time. We were all within a year or two of each other, and, as we were demobbed in age groups, we tended to be drawn together. We had just won the war and were slightly aggressive and abrasive, and bursting with new ideas. The Goons wanted to produce a revolutionary form of humour; and they did. It took time, and despite their many critics they proved they were right.'

Their last producer, John Browell, a man who weighs words as carefully as a prospector weighing gold dust, spent eight years with the team. 'No other show has ever matched it for complexity or multiplicity. When it first started everyone said it was pretty awful, rowdy, undisciplined and noisy. It was ahead of its time. You can't take the public by the scruff of the neck and shake them like a dog and make them like it. The fighting to reach the top was hard, but we made it.'

For Browell they were hilarious, exhausting shows, with lunacy mingling with sheer genius, but 'a great deal more satisfying and closer to reality than anything else I have ever produced.'

Few people are better qualified to give a touch-line view of the birth and development of The Goons than James Thomas, television critic of the old *News Chronicle* who now holds a similar position with the *Daily Express*.

'In a way I was the midwife at the birth of The Goons, and it happened in the Grafton Arms one night when a quartet not very well known had gone for a drink. When I joined them I had never heard of them and the BBC had kept them very carefully under wraps. The BBC was then very wary of any new form of humour. But the four were determined to make a brand new mark. I was very impressed with their ideas and decided to write about them. I did not think my Editor, at that time Robert Cruickshank, a distinguished Washington correspondent and brilliant editor, would be very interested in my story, but he was. And indeed, with the vision that he always had he realized that here was something very special. So I can claim to have written the very first article about The Goons.

'But back to the pub. Sellers at the time was the man in the spotlight with his impersonations. The man moving the whole thing forward was Milligan. There was also Bentine, who was later to find himself at odds with Milligan, and to leave The Goons and go on and make a name for himself. In the pub, Secombe drew me his first impression of what a Goon should look like. This was a little line drawing which later appeared in the paper and has since been tragically lost. This is a great pity, for over these many years of comedy it would be invaluable. I remember the four going into the snack bar and taking four knives and doing a sword dance while they sang wildly, to the astonishment of the regulars. It was a Goon Show preview.

'Between them they introduced a revolution in comedy. All four went on to become stars in their own right, but the strange thing is they never forgot those birth pangs over the beer. And neither, of course, will I as a critic. Because there was here the germ of something very special that went beyond the ideas born in the old Music Halls and even by Hollywood's top film writers. From that chance meeting there came an incredible amount of publicity which put on the map four people who were to influence comedy for at least two decades on both sides of the Atlantic. We have come all the way from The Goons as far as Monty Python, and John Cleese acknowledges how much today's crazy comedy owes to them. None of the four originals can ever forget that chance meeting with me at the Grafton. It would have happened anyway, but I like to think I helped to get on a show of which the BBC were really apprehensive. The first show which I attended shocked some BBC executives, but it had the audiences rolling in the aisles. A new era in radio comedy had begun.

'Come back? Possibly. There is among the originals still a tremendous feeling of what was achieved by that breakthrough. Now, of course, they do not need to go back to the hard slog of the Goon Shows. Though their humour, in my opinion, would still be very acceptable in a dull world of TV comedy made up of so many trashy situation comedies.'

The men themselves?

'Secombe, fat and happy, producing at the drop of a hat his Goon language, a man who cannot forget that past.

'Sellers has gone on to be a top film star and has grown away from the other world of comedy.

'Bentine went on to put forward his own ideas, some successful, some not; but he always seems to be a little bitter about his parting from people who went on to be superstars.

'Milligan. What do you say about Spike?

'He perhaps was the most vulnerable of all, but he has survived very well and no one should ever forget that it was his words which made it all possible.'

In the history of British comedy, the Crazy Gang are perhaps the only others who have approached the cult proportions of The Goons, but their humour was hardly cerebral and didn't attempt to achieve anything but laughter. The late Bud Flanagan, a straw-hatted clown in the classic tradition, said, 'I've followed The Goons ever since they started on the air. In fact, I've watched their careers very carefully, and I'm one of their biggest champions. They're brilliant especially Peter Sellers. We're crazy, but their humour is far more advanced than ours.'

Mr Con Mahoney, Head of Light Entertainment, BBC Radio, believes that one day a familiar blue plaque will be cemented into the frontage of the Grafton Arms proclaiming, 'Goonery was brewed here.'

He said: 'The success of the Goons' approach to comedy depended on the complete involvement of the whole team in every aspect of the production. In writing terms, Barry Took and Marty Feldman came closest to reproducing the flavour of such humour in areas of their scripts for "Round The Horne", but this "team" creativity did not re-emerge in the media until some ten years after the Goons had first baffled the radio planners. Those responsible this time were the groups of young writer/performers in the University revue field, anxious to break new ground, whose school and college listening had undoubtedly been seasoned with Goon humour, and from these we got the radio series "I'm Sorry, I'll Read That Again", and a spate of highly original television developments.

'In a sense the wheel has come full circle, because surely the Goons sought to contrive for the special requirements of radio an approach which has its origins in the richly unconventional visual teamwork of groups such as the Marx Brothers and our own Crazy Gang.

'In style, the writers achieved the most distinctive form of humour created by BBC radio. Whereas realism was plainly discernible in the work of "Hancock's Half-Hour", "Take It From Here", "Much Binding" and most other brands of thirty-minute comedy shows the Goon Show alone was pure fantasy.'

More detached but no less enthusiastic are the views of Prince Charles, one of the trio's most dedicated and knowledgeable fans who sees an 'eternal quality' in their humour. In his foreword to *More Goon Show Scripts** which His Royal Highness has given his permission to quote, he says:

'No matter how much "the fashion" in humour changes, there will always be thousands of people whose minds are attuned to the kind of mental slapstick and imaginary cartoonery that typifies Goonery. For that reason I am always hoping that many more Goon shows in record form will be made available to their dotty and devoted supporters.'

The important thing about Prince Charles's words is that they are so far removed from the normal platitudes of a Royal endorsement. They are warm, and enter into the whole spirit of Goonery. Who could have envisaged jokes about the Royal Family being countered by jokes from the heir apparent?

In his 'Backword' to the same book, Secombe, the least complex of the three, never ceases to be amazed that even today when each has achieved individual fame they are still referred to in the Press as 'ex-Goon' or 'arch-Goon'.

'It seems that old Goons, like old soldiers, never die, and show little signs of fading away,' he says, before turning aside to giggle and add, that in his own case a little fading away would not be out of place.

One almost detects a note of awe when he seeks to explain

* *More Goon Show Scripts* (Woburn Press).

his views. 'There is a quality of indestructability in Spike's creations which seems to defy the normal processes of Nature. If ever, or whenever, the Big Bang comes, I have the feeling that the dreadful silence which follows it will be broken by a dishevelled Eccles rising Phoenix-like from the ashes saying, "How about Dat?" And as they disappear hand in hand over the horizon there will be cries of "Wait for me", as Bloodnok, Gryptype, Neddie and company emerge from their hiding places to go bounding after them. They might then create a lunatic new world which would be infinitely preferable to the old one.'

The depth of Secombe's feelings seem to belie his often repeated claim that to him the shows were never more than a good giggle.

Few stars have written or said as much about themselves as Sellers, so in theory he should be an open book. Alas! the opposite is true! He's like the man who sees a perfect reflection of himself on the surface of the pond and can't resist tossing a pebble in.

One minute he is a colourless, introvert, hiding beneath the skin of a self-created character; the next he is a dominant perfectionist who not only knows himself but also the clear path he has to tread.

He is not being intentionally evasive or obscure. The seeming contradictions make sense: he does have chameleon-like qualities.

He sees nothing inconsistent in telling stories that seem to cancel each other out. It reminds one of those old-fashioned photographs which when you pressed the edges completely altered the portrait, so that one second you had a smiling benign countenance, the next a grim, foreboding visage. It was still the same picture, though.

But if he ever does hide behind someone else's face you can be sure there is a very good reason for it.

He loves to recount the story of when he was a teenager and getting nowhere with his equally young date. 'I had taken her to see Robert Donat in "Knight Without Armour" at the Odeon, Swiss Cottage, and I was wildly trying to impress her. When she came out she said, "Oh, I'm so mad about Donat". I could imitate him, and I did. It was a great success.'

A trivial, insignificant incident, except the story has a sequel, for many years later Sellers was Donat's neighbour in Highgate Village, London, and one day he saw his idol on the balcony and asked if he could photograph him. Donat obliged, but as he operated the camera Sellers could not help thinking, 'If only you knew what I once did in your name.'

At times he likes to foster the belief that he is without a real identity. When a man stopped him in a restaurant to ask 'You are Peter Sellers, aren't you?' he replied, 'Not today,' and walked off.

Yet he can still be very tetchy if outsiders talk about the faceless Sellers.

Peter insists, 'I know him very well indeed. Sometimes he bores me, sometimes he frightens me. Frequently he bewilders me. Occasionally he astonishes me, and sometimes I think he's mad.'

Clouseau-like, he collects clues about himself, then scatters them in such a way that renders a solution virtually impossible. As a Virgoan, for instance, he says that he is obsessively tidy and thus he tends to compartmentalize everything and everybody. Except, of course, himself.

'I have,' he once confessed, 'the reputation for being a shit, but it's a reputation mostly put about by those mediocre people who will always resent and try to cut down a man's talent. Spike Milligan says, and God knows he's right, the world is full up with mediocrity, and you'll find it everywhere, and when you brush with it, you brush up venom.'

Conversely, of course, it is only the mediocrity of the majority's talent that makes people like Sellers outstanding. Hence the admiration. Is Sellers reluctant to accept that because it could lead to a charge of arrogance?

Certainly there is total dedication to his art; as we know, when he prepares for a new role he assumes a monastic aloofness. As he told his friend Kretzmer, 'I walk around, trying different accents, feeling my way to the character. I do this every time. I stare at my own image in the mirror every morning, waiting for the other fellow – the man I'm going to portray – to emerge, and stare back at me. I am waiting for this stranger to come into my life. When it happens, I have this flush of happiness.'

Added Kretzmer, 'In fact, so complete is this surrender to the role, that even the structure of Sellers' features appear to undergo physical changes...'

Dennis Main Wilson has also observed these physical transformations. He rates Sellers as 'probably the greatest all-round performer the world has had this century,' adding: 'He's a fine comedian, a brilliant actor who always puts great truth into his performance, and a marvellous technician as well. He's a genius, with a temperament like a highly tuned string; that makes him a difficult blighter to work with.'

Behind the total absorption, Wilson sees a frightened man. 'Peter is terrified of losing his talent. He keeps asking himself, "How long will the public keep laughing at me, or for me?" And because his gifts are so great he has so much more to lose than most men.'

John Browell endorses what Kretzmer says. 'Peter comes to life when he can turn into another character. When he played Crun you could see him becoming thin and ancient. He is a marvellous man.'

Eric Sykes, the gangling comedian who is also one of the finest script writers in the business, said, 'He is one of the world's greatest character actors. Greater even than Alec Guiness.'

One of his earlier films was 'The Ladykillers', and he's certainly been that in real life. And throughout his three marriages and numerous affairs he has never found a lasting relationship. Yet his former loves still talk warmly and loyally about him, as do his many male friends who have been driven to near distraction. Britt Ekland went through a tempestuous marriage, but admitted, 'I would do it again,' whilst model Titi Wachtmeister, whose three-year romance ended volcanically in 1975, said, 'Being with him is like living with twenty different men. He's nice and sweet one minute, and the next he's in a dreadful mood. It has been quite a tumultuous three years, I can tell you.'

Sophia Loren, who like Sellers had known the hard times before the good, said, 'Many people think he is a shallow man because of his effortless impersonations. In fact, he is very deep, and anything he says makes sense.'

Harry Secombe who always talks good horse sense, said, 'He's quite the most extraordinary man I'm ever likely to meet. I'm sure he would be capable of doing anything he cares to undertake. And I don't only mean mimicry. Whenever he starts something, whether it is a new part or a new hobby, he is not happy until he has mastered it. Everything must be just right. He's the greatest perfectionist I have ever known. Every new part allows him to explore yet another new area of his talent, and he is often surprised to discover how far his talent can stretch. I don't think he will ever stop stretching.'

Milligan's assessment of Sellers is, well, typically Spike. His compliments end up with him patting his own back. He loves to talk about their 'love-hate', 'Gilbert and Sullivan', 'oil and water' relationship before readily acknowledging Sellers' great talent.

'We have a completely opposite approach to what we want to do, but by hammering it out we come to some agreement. But it's hellish going. When we get together we smoulder. When we talk to each other over the phone there's always at the back of our minds the thought: "You're wrong, and you bloody well know you're wrong."

'You see, I'm deeper than he is. He takes things seriously, but in quite a different way. I think he's perfectly aware, too, of the state of homo sapiens, but he thinks, "What's the use?" He doesn't think deeper than that. I think humanity's a failure, but he doesn't care to think about that. I think he's an enigma; he is to me and I don't think he understands how much talent he has got. We always clash about the quality of perfection we want to achieve. I think I'm a greater perfectionist than he is, where the production of ideas is concerned.'

On one occasion, Spike said that Peter enjoyed his fame but had remained unchanged by his wealth. On another he said that money had made him 'miserable and morose'.

It depends, really, how you like you eggs – sunny side up or sunny side down!

One could go on quoting opinions and impressions without getting any nearer the truth. Producing a portrait of Sellers is rather like making up one of those Photofit pictures the police use for the purpose of identity. Just when everything seems to have slotted perfectly into place some niggling doubt arises. It's almost right but some vital, indefinable element is missing, so that the end result is just a shadow of the real thing.

Of one thing, however, we can be sure. The Goon Show years were the happiest and most enjoyable in Sellers' long and distinguished career. He has never hedged on that.

Milligan is a far less complicated person than Sellers and an indignant Spike would be the first to disagree with that. But somehow or other the thousands of cliches used to explain his personality fit him like a pair of hand-made gloves. He *is* a 'tormented genius', life *is* either 'agony or ecstasy', behind the greying beard *is* the face of a 'broken hearted clown'. Life *is* a 'vale of tears' only made bearable by the God-given gift for making others laugh.

To lesser mortals his fears and phobias are incomprehensible. The man on the production line at Ford's can't even begin to understand how a man can be so miserable doing what he loves and getting rich in the process. But Spike can. What's more, he can be as eloquently convincing explaining how miserable he would be if he wasn't doing it.

Spike has repeatedly written and spoken of the tremendous strain he underwent when writing the Goon Shows, and when Peter Sellers was recently asked about it he said, 'I don't know why he did it for so long in that case.'

It was not an uncharitable observation, he was simply trying to answer a question objectively. He has never made any secret of his own intense dislike of the theatre because of its repetitive nature, therefore he could not understand why a friend should remain with a show which was slowly crucifying him.

'I see Spike as a brilliant writer-actor who could never make up his mind whether he wanted to act or write. He has improved enormously over the years as an actor. But he, Harry and I – he and I especially – have had a love-hate relationship over a long period. He is much warmer towards Harry. His compliments, if he ever gives one, are always two-edged. I think he feels that all the things that have happened to Harry and me in the way of success, should possibly have gone to him. He feels as if he did not get a fair share of the pie. But he is very successful. He is a genius, that man.'

Two-edged compliments!

But they still continue to meet as regularly as their personal commitments allow, and the get-togethers are hilarious occasions for they immediately lapse into the fantasy world of The Goons, where only the love side of their relationship is remembered.

'I disagree with Spike that tomorrow can never be as happy as yesterday. I live for today and tomorrow. He lives in a permanent nostalgia,' said Sellers.

Sykes is more sympathetic to the strain imposed on Milligan by the script writing: 'He did on his own a job which would normally be handled by six or seven men.'

The Observer, not normally given to writing in-depth articles on radio comedians, described Milligan as 'a satirist with a bitter laugh' and credits him as 'the thinkng power' behind The Goons. It is important towards an appreciation of Milligan, for part of his torment was due to the fact that he was never satisfied with simply raising laughter, there had to be an object and purpose for his wit. The word *message* wouldn't even be out of place. His sights were always aimed at a specific target, and the target was invariably pomposity or some hidebound aspect of the Establishment.

Michael Foot, the zealous political reformer, once remarked, 'Spike Milligan is my favourite anarchist, in the

179

most respectable way, of course. And I mean it as the highest possible tribute to the man.'

Dennis Main Wilson thinks Spike's India-upbringing is the key to it all. 'He was anti-officer, anti-elitist, and anti all establishments. That kind often end up creating their own establishment, and Spike is no exception. He has a God-given driving force, or whatever you care to call it, which means that however many times he is down – and he has been down a few times – he has never been beaten. The fact that he is Irish is very important. They are not only a different race to the English, but different to all the other Celts. They have a great gift for fantasy. You can see it in Yeats, Shaw, O'Casey and Milligan. They can also be a devious race in so far as they don't like to face up to the truth.'

John Browell was reluctant to talk at length about the pressure of the scripts on Milligan. 'Spike says they were the cause of his break-up, but some writers turn out scripts week after week without a breakdown. Spike said the BBC put too much pressure on him, but the pressure was not all that enormous. He doesn't really like the BBC and tends to bite the hand that feeds him. He likes me as a producer, but as I am BBC also, he doesn't like me as a person. It really depends on what hat he sees me wearing.'

Browell, a charming, almost diffident man when it comes to expressing his own views of other people, said, 'Spike? He is a lot of things. You can't describe him in a few words. He is a near genius, and I don't use superlatives easily, I am very conservative in descriptions. He's not easy to work or live with. But he has moments of great charm and tenderness, and gets involved in good deeds. One wonders, sometimes, how deeply, or whether it is a platform for his own ideas. It is difficult to know when it's genuine or whether he's putting on an act. He fluctuates from agony to ecstasy.'

The Rev. Fred Secombe tells an illuminating story about Spike which reveals how he used humour as a vehicle for saying something he felt deeply about. In this case it was the empty promises of the politicians.

'Sellers, Harry and Bentine went out with Milligan one day and Spike suddenly got up on a stool and started making an election speech, the theme of which was "Vote Plantagenet". It was near Piccadilly, I believe. Anyway, a few people gathered around, and Milligan said how he would abolish taxes, and made a lot of marvellous promises. At the end he said: "Now my followers will hand out leaflets, which I hope you will take home and read, as they explain what my Plantagenet plan is all about." Then the others solemnly proceeded to hand out old theatre bills. Of course, people didn't know what had hit them.'

It wasn't an isolated incident. Sometimes he would enter a restaurant, suddenly jump on a chair and shout 'Vote Plantagenet' a couple of times, then calmly sit down and carry on eating. It was funny, at the same time it was a gesture of protest.

Not all his pranks were in that vein. Sometimes they had a Chaplinesque humour-tinged sadness about them, as on the occasion he was strolling through Hyde Park and saw a rippling-muscled statue of a Greek god. He rolled up his sleeve, climbed on to the plinth, and felt its biceps with a look of envy. Then he felt his own, shook his head sadly, came back down, put on his jacket and walked slowly away. The small crowd of eight or nine people which had gathered watched with utter amazement. Not a word had been spoken; there had been no need – Spike's simple mime had spoken volumes.

The Rev. Secombe recalls his very first meeting with Spike which shows how Spike was easily swept away on the waves of his own fantasies. 'Harry was at The Palace, Chelsea, doing Widow Twankey in "Aladdin", and he invited my wife, Connie, and me to London to see him. After the show he took us out for a meal. At one stage we were left sitting with Spike who launched into a very sad, harrowing tale, about his upbringing in Ireland – how he came from a peasant family, and how they had hardly any food to live on, and sat on boxes when men came to take away the furniture. We were practically in tears when Harry returned and stopped him in mid flow. "You bloody liar" he said, and explained how Milligan had been brought up in India and was a stranger to Ireland. But he was so convincing, and, of course, we had never met him before.'

Spike is a past master at weaving such make-believe sagas. But if at the end his audience are made aware of the true situation the nagging doubt remains that Spike still believes his own story.

Sometimes a simple incident tells us more about a person than volumes of words. When Oscar Wilde told the customs in America, 'I have nothing to declare but my genius,' it summed him up perfectly.

In the same way that rather tragi-comic scene at the Camden Theatre involving a sockful of custard may tell us all we need to know, or all we will ever know, about Milligan.

Harry Secombe? If the world was full of such people the psychologists would be joining the dole queue. The repetitive Gertrude Stein could perfectly sum him up: Secombe is Secombe, is Secombe, is Secombe...

Peter Sellers said, 'Harry is one of the few people I know about whom I've never heard anything bad. He's a great clown, a great singer, and a truly wonderful fellow in his typically Welsh way. He's consistently sane and one of life's leading optimists.'

After that there isn't much left to say. You could canvass half the theatrical profession for an opinion of Secombe, and although the words would be different the sentiments would be the same.

Sellers loves to tell a story which he thinks personifies Harry's charm and attitude to life. Secombe had just been stopped by a police car for speeding through Kingston, and when he lowered his window the officer said: 'I suppose you know, sir, that you were exceeding 60 m.p.h.?'

'Yes,' said Harry smiling sunnily, 'and a beautiful day it is for it, isn't it?'

Main Wilson said, 'Harry has never changed, and never will. Everybody loves him, and that's not said glibly. He's a very Christian man with a tremendous dynamic force. He's as straight as a die, and totally honest in his work and to his friends.' He paused there as if trying desperately hard to find some small fault that would lift him out of the haloed bracket. 'Deep inside, he is terribly nervous. I think the giggle gives a clue.'

The late Godfrey Winn found him a big man in every sense of the word. 'Mind you, this man who hasn't an enemy in the world can be serious too, as when he talks about his ambitions to be respected as an author as well as a comedian and singer. He creates optimism around him. That's his magic.'

Lynda Lee-Potter, the *Daily Mail* writer whose pen can often resemble sharpened talons, was completely captivated. 'If anybody in Show Business is ill or down on his luck, Harry Secombe is always the first one to be there with a cheque, a helping hand, or the offer of a job. He is a man of extraordinary talent, but he has never got bigheaded. He is humble and kind, and even now still a bit shattered that life has turned out so marvellously well.'

It's because he is so natural and so easy to get on with that Harry hasn't attracted the attention of the open-up-and-probe school of writers to quite the same extent as Spike and Peter. When the lid of the casket is lifted, they know exactly what they'll find.

The harshest criticisms have come from Harry himself, who will admit that in his early days conceit egged him on to do anything for a laugh – even balancing a packet of tea on his nose in a crowded supermarket. 'But you reach a stage in the profession where you are accepted for what you are and can respond normally to anyone you meet.'

So much has been said about Sellers' and Milligan's obsessive pursuit of perfection that Harry has tended to be thrust into the background as the amiable, larger-than-life buffoon who simply uses his head for a hat rack. Most people think his comedy is an extension of himself and comes without any effort or study. In fact, his timing and technique only seem so natural because they are the result of years of hard graft and observation.

No doubt he would hide behind one of his hysterical giggles if you mentioned the word perfectionist in his presence, but his brother Fred has no such inhibitions. 'He is a perfectionist in his own way. If he has an audience of 1,000 and can see that two people are not laughing, he worries about those two and wonders why they don't find him funny. When he watches himself on television he looks for the mistakes in order to improve his performance next time. He says that a man who is fully satisfied with his work is finished.'

It is not only in his professional life that he has this sense of dedication. When he took up golf he got down to single figures. When he began to write he wanted to be read for his words, not just his name. The same applied when he took up horse riding.

Without the vast comforting bulk of Harry Donald Secombe, The Goons might not have lasted as long as they have, for he certainly acted as a stabilizing buttress on the more explosive Sellers and Milligan. By the same standards, however, if the three had all been as alike as peas in a pod there would have been no Goons in the first place.

Their strength was that although they are so totally dissimilar as individuals, they shared the same crazy wavelength. Because of that, they have together produced more lasting laughter than any other comedians this country has ever known.

As Secombe would remark: 'Who could want a better epitaph?'

Chapter Ten

GOON FOR GOOD?

Since that last recording in the old Camden Theatre in 1972, barely a week has passed without some newspaper carrying an item heralding the return of The Goons, and with each announcement the controversy grows as to whether it would be a wonderful thing or a gross error of judgement. Meanwhile, the three men who could supply the once-and-for-all answer seem reluctant to administer the *coup de grace*. When faced with the inevitable question – will there be any more? – they tend to give a yes, no, maybe, reply. They remind one of three indecisive bathers standing at the water's edge testing the temperature with their big toes, never quite sure whether to take the plunge or not.

For the millions of Goon fans, who would welcome them back tomorrow, it is all rather frustrating, even irritating. They feel like the judge awaiting the return of a jury, which has been out for several hours, growing ever more impatient as the hours tick past without a decision, and fearing all the time that there'll be a disagreement. Reared in a society where the dictum 'supply and demand' has held sway for so long, they can't understand the prevarication. There's certainly the demand, as anyone who takes the trouble to ring up the BBC will find out, and as for the supply, The Goons frequently hint that it is there ready and waiting to be delivered.

The astonishing thing is that the clamour for a return is still as strong as it was sixteen years ago when the series officially ended. It is hard to recall such loyal devotion in the whole history of entertainment.

As recently as January 1976, when The Goons were presented with a silver disc for selling 70,000 copies of their LP The Last Goon Show of All – worth £75,000 – Peter Sellers hinted at a comeback. 'There is a chance we may do another,' he said.

There was no holding back the photographers at the celebration get-together where the trio automatically lapsed into Goonery. And those few words of Sellers' were enough to send the journalists rampaging down memory lane. The *Evening News*, under a headline 'Goon, but certainly not forgotten', enthused about the event and took the opportunity to remind readers what they were missing.

'Great news Ned lad! Pause while plausible public school

185

type villain Gryptype-Thynne recovers breath and Crown Jewels.

'Yes, it's true folks, Seagoon, liquorice-and-string-hero Blue-bottle; Eccles, born 1863, with 18,312 interviews but no jobs; and Major Bloodnok, Indian Army Rtd., military idiot, coward and bar – have won a silver disc...'

If the latest pop idol had won the award it would have rated no more than a couple of lines down-column; The Goons got extensive coverage. And emphasizing the magnetic attraction of the shows the occasion was used as an opportunity to renew the speculation about a return.

A BBC spokesman was quoted as saying, 'There seems to be more interest in The Goons than ever. We have been releasing an album of Goon shows every year and plan to carry on if The Goons agree.'

Sellers was then a multi-million pound property, Secombe probably the biggest name in television and stage light entertainment, while Milligan had no equal as a one-man-band. Yet the *Evening News* preferred to use a 1951 picture of them in their Goon heyday.

It wasn't an isolated revival of interest. Only the previous year the BBC had done a series of repeat programmes – chiefly for the benefit of younger listeners who had never heard them. Spike Milligan had been mainly responsible, for he had contacted the BBC's Director General, Sir Charles Curran, and told him of the vast interest The Goons commanded in all spheres of life.

Said his manager Norma Farnes, 'The idea came to Spike after he had been touring universities with his one-man revue "For One Week Only". After the shows he met hundreds of students, and they nearly all asked about the 'Goon Shows' and whether there would ever be a chance of hearing them. He was quite bowled over by the thought that all these youngsters – they must have been around six when the programmes first went out – had even heard of them.'

John Browell who produced the shows for so long, said, 'We've had thousands of letters, many from young people, asking us to bring them back.'

For the cynics who heard the tinkle of cash registers when they learned of Spike's approach, it must be pointed out that he, Sellers and Secombe offered to waive the repeat fees.

Although the BBC still has a lot of shows in the archives, this doesn't stop the incessant demand for new shows. While the repeats are always welcomed by devotees, they would much prefer more original scripts. Certainly Milligan continues to hold out hope for the starved fans. 'I would like to do more Goon Show Specials. But the biggest problem of all is getting us all available and together at the same time. I might be off to Australia, Peter in America, and Harry in Spain. And even if we were all in England at the same time, we're usually tied up on our own projects. We have, after all, gone our different ways over the past few years. When I had to write a Goon Show every week, it was an incredible strain, but writing a one-off is a different matter. That is more a labour of love. We had as much fun with "The Last Goon Show of All" as we had in the old days.'

So the door is still not finally closed on more Goon Shows, although it is extremely unlikely that there will be any more long-running series. The 50th Anniversary broadcast revealed how quickly The Goons can get a show together, but even more important, how they can enjoy it.

A frequently heard argument is that the real obstacle to any regular return is money: the BBC just couldn't afford to pay Milligan, Sellers and Secombe the kind of fees they can now command. Fortunately, it's an argument that doesn't stand up to scrutiny. The Goons are big money spinners. The original 'Ying Tong Song' sold 280,000 copies when it was first released, and sixteen years later it was back in the hit parade. Secombe greeted the news with, 'It's like Ben Hur winning the Grand Prix.' Apart from that, any book by, or about The Goons automatically rockets into the best seller lists. There have been books of scripts, a book on their correspondence and doodles, while Harry's life story was appropriately titled *Goon for Lunch*. Milligan, surprised at

187

the never ending demand, said, 'I suppose they'll be doing the Goons' Laundry List next.'

It's not such a far-fetched idea. When you can advertise in the medical journal *The Lancet* – 'The Goons are contagious. Infect a loved one this Christmas' – you can get away with anything.

One Swedish bookseller placed a large order for the 'Go-on' book thinking it was a sex-manual.

Still on the subject of money, there is a considerable interest abroad in anything appertaining to The Goons. South Africa and Australia which bought the old programmes are still running them, and there are long queues at the book stalls. The cheque books would soon be out if a new series hove in sight.

Quite apart from all that, Sellers is not motivated by money; as he has so often said he is not interested in being the richest man in the cemetery. Anyway, what is money to him? 'The Return of the Pink Panther', the second in the Inspector Clouseau series, is one of the biggest money making comedies in film history, and for his part in the follow up 'The Pink Panther Strikes Again', he is said to have received £625,000. With that kind of money you don't have to start worrying about wallpaper.

There is, however, a much more valid argument against a come-back. Some chroniclers of the entertainment scene have stated unequivocally that a return would be disastrous. Times have changed, comedy has progressed, and a return to purely aural comedy, after people have become accustomed to 'Monty Python' and 'The Goodies' would be a retrograde step.

As William Davis, the editor of *Punch*, put it: 'Turning the clock back might be fun for a while but it could also be a bad mistake. The Goons are part of an era, a delightful memory. Why spoil it?'

Author David Nathan, in his revealing book *The Laughter-maker*, a review of post-war comedy, touched on the same point. The Goons came about, he said, through Milligan's dislike of regimentation – something shared by nearly everybody who suffered from the war. It was a perceptive assessment. But one must disagree with Nathan when he goes on to say, 'If Spike had written The Goon Show at any other time it wouldn't have worked!'

With apologies to Wordsworth, but not Nathan, many feel the rallying cry today should be: 'Milligan! England hath need of thee...'

The time is ripe for a return.

When the pound has sunk so far that even Moriarty would find it difficult stooping low enough to pick it up, when personal freedom is gradually being eroded, when civil servants juggle with unacceptable figures until they become palatable, and politicians have made double-talk the official language of Westminster, there is a greater need than ever for Spike's incisive satire. If we are going to be taken for a ride, they say, at least let us laugh on the journey and poke the finger of fun at the driver.

They argue that the return of The Goons is in the National interest. A return to intentional insanity is long overdue. As Vincent Mulchrone commented so many years ago, the world they created was a lot better than the one politicians have lumbered us with. Remember that very first Goon Show of all? It ended with:

Bentine: And so Britain has struggled valiantly on through the post-war years, fighting for a better standard of life, for the pursuit of happiness, for freedom ... Fighting for her very existence! Until today the Motherland can still raise her proud face to the skies and say...

Secombe: HEELLLPPPP ! ! !

Affluent or effluent days, The Goons' message is still valid. They have achieved a permanency that is as much a part of the British scene as the Tower of London or Cheddar Cheese. You've only got to switch on to 'Now Who Do You Do?' to realize that today's crop of talented impressionists have no intention whatsoever of letting The Goons vanish from the scene.

Having said all that, one senses that the final decision will rest with Peter Sellers, not because he is more, or less, important than the other two, but simply because he is so un-decided. Milligan seems agreeable, providing it doesn't become a chore; while Secombe, being the man he is, is quite willing to fall in with their wishes. He just wants to make people laugh.

So what are the chances of Sellers giving a firm decision?

When he was in London making his latest Pink Panther film he kindly agreed to be interviewed in his luxury flat high above London's Victoria. He was recovering from a bout of the 'flu, but rather than cancel the appointment – he was due to start filming next morning and if he called it off it would have been weeks before he was again available – he sat up in bed and talked.

It was the kind of generous gesture which makes it diffi-cult for anyone to accept some of the unpleasant things he has said about himself and which others have said about him. In a surprisingly small bedroom he talked frankly and earnestly, never trying to evade a question. He talked of his religious beliefs, his interest in clairvoyancy, yoga, how he sees himself, and of the real pleasure those Goon Show days provided.

It was only when he was asked about the possibility of the three getting together again that he seemed hesitant. 'We do get together every now and then and have a good time,' he said.

But workwise?

'They are two great colleagues and always will be. But I don't think there will be any more series. Harry is very busy, but I could work with him. Spike has this enormous ego these days and it would be difficult to work with it. He seems to be uniquely jealous of me as a person. He is much warmer towards Harry.'

Still Sellers refuses to pull down the shutters completely. Difficult doesn't mean impossible; and no more *series* doesn't mean no more *shows*. But he doesn't elaborate. In any case, the doctor was due.

Sellers' beautifully furnished apartment mirrors his course through life. There is a framed picture of him as the bigoted

Kite; on a small table there is a photograph he took of the Queen Mother and Prince Charles; the zany side is reflected in a pair of battered, tatty tennis shoes mounted in an ornate frame. There are lots of Goon pictures and a spotlight projects a Yoga sign on to a wall below which Sellers does his morning exercises and meditation. A huge panoramic window runs the whole length of the lounge, and in the centre is a powerful telescope mounted on a tripod.

If swivelled to the left it can be focussed on Buckingham Palace, to the right on The Grafton Arms public house. A ninety degree arc encompasses the rise from pub entertainer to friend of Royalty.

Perhaps the spirit of Dan Leno will one day urge him into a return to The Goons. If it does, so much the better.

If not, perhaps one morning he will focus the telescope on to Buckingham Palace and receive a Royal Command in semaphore from one of his most devoted fans, Prince Charles, RN.

That failing, perhaps he will, in a fit of nostalgia, put The Grafton Arms in fine focus and bring back such a flood of happy memories that he will be prepared to bury his misgivings and give so many millions what they want.

A return of The Goons.

Armchair bookshop

All good bookshops stock Everest titles. If you have any difficulty getting our books – or if you prefer to shop from home – please fill in this form.

☐ VALENTINO – THE LOVE GOD Botham & Donnelly   93p

☐ LAST SNOWS OF SPRING Ken Johnson   68p

☐ CROSSROADS 1 – A NEW BEGINNING
Malcolm Hulke   58p

☐ CROSSROADS 2 – A WARM BREEZE Malcolm Hulke   63p

☐ CROSSROADS 3 – SOMETHING OLD, SOMETHING NEW
Malcolm Hulke   68p

☐ CROSSROADS 4 – A TIME FOR LIVING
Malcolm Hulke   73p

☐ THE CRIME COMMANDOS Peter Cave   68p

☐ THE OLYMPIC MISSION Pamela Ferguson   78p

☐ A SPY FOR CHURCHILL Robert Vacha   78p

☐ PHANTOMS OVER POTSDAM Robert Vacha   78p

☐ HUNTERS' WALK Willis & Hart   83p

NAME ....

ADDRESS ....

....